Dyslexia and Inclusion

Now fully updated, *Dyslexia and Inclusion* aims to equip all teachers with the necessary knowledge of dyslexia in order to for it to be effectively understood and dealt with in the classroom.

The book is based around Reid's five signposts for successful inclusion - acknowledging differences, recognizing strengths, understanding what is meant by inclusion, planning for practice, and ensuring that the task outcomes are attainable. In identifying the key issues of inclusive practice, the book details current research whilst also providing support to meet the practical needs of the classroom teacher. This highly practical, topical and accessible text includes chapters on:

- Effective learning.
- Curriculum access and differentiation.
- Whole school approaches.
- Specific approaches in reading, spelling, writing and numeracy.

By understanding the crucial aspects of dyslexia, teachers can be proactive and anticipate the type of difficulties they may encounter. This book will be beneficial to all teachers looking to support their students with dyslexia and help them to fulfil their potential in school and in the wider community.

Gavin Reid is an international consultant on teaching and learning in the Middle East, Europe and the UK. He is also an educational psychologist based in Vancouver, Canada and has published extensively in the field of dyslexia, literacy, motivation and learning. He was formerly a Senior Lecturer at the University of Edinburgh and Visiting Professor at the University of British Columbia in Vancouver.

Dyslexia and Inclusion
Classroom approaches for assessment, teaching and learning

Second edition

Gavin Reid

Routledge
Taylor & Francis Group

LONDON AND NEW YORK

First published 2006
by Routledge
2 Park Square, Milton Park, Abingdon, Oxon OX14 4RN

This second edition published 2013

Simultaneously published in the USA and Canada
by Routledge
711 Third Avenue, New York, NY 10017

Routledge is an imprint of the Taylor & Francis Group, an informa business

British Library Cataloguing in Publication Data
A catalogue record for this book is available from the British Library

Library of Congress Cataloging in Publication Data
Reid, Gavin, 1950-
Dyslexia and inclusion : classroom approaches for assessment, teaching and learning / by Gavin Reid. -- 2nd ed.
p. cm.
ISBN 978-0-415-60758-2 (pbk.) -- ISBN 978-0-203-10883-3 (ebook) 1. Dyslexic children--Education. 2. Inclusive education. I. Title.
LC4708.R452 2012
371.91'44--dc23
2012001398

ISBN: 978-0-415-60758-2 (pbk)
ISBN: 978-0-203-10883-3 (ebk)

Typeset in Helvetica
by Saxon Graphics Ltd, Derby

MIX
Paper from
responsible sources
FSC
www.fsc.org   FSC® C004839

Printed and bound in Great Britain by the MPG Books Group

Contents

Introduction

Since the first edition a great deal of progress has been made in embedding dyslexia-friendly policies and practices into mainstream education. Research and government policies in the UK, USA, Canada, Australia and New Zealand are providing a sharp edge to the need to provide full curricular access to all and eradicate any disparity and inequality in meeting the needs of students such as those with dyslexia. There is still a need for specialist programmes but teachers in mainstream primary and secondary still have a major role to play. It is important that they equip themselves with the knowledge and the understanding of dyslexia, what it is, how it is recognised and importantly how it can be effectively dealt with.

In the first edition I acknowledged five signposts for successful inclusion. These were acknowledging differences, recognizing strengths, understanding what is meant by inclusion, planning for practice, and ensuring that the task outcomes are attainable. These points still hold true today. It is the intention of this book to develop and extend these points substantially and to indicate very clearly that the needs of students with dyslexia can and should be met in mainstream education. To achieve this however there needs to be a significant redesign of training to ensure that dyslexia and the other specific difficulties are considered and placed high on the agenda in training courses, both undergraduate and postgraduate, and play a major role in schools' ongoing professional development programmes.

I hope this book can play a part in this area of development and that the ideas, strategies and resources highlighted in this book can prove to be beneficial to all, supporting students with dyslexia and helping them fulfil their potential in school and in the wider community.

Dr Gavin Reid
Vancouver, Canada January 2012

1 Dyslexia

This chapter discusses the following:

- Definitions and characteristics
- Policies
- Government initiatives and reports
- Research and implications for practice
- Teaching provision.

Introduction

'Inclusion' is a term that has international currency. Every country is now striving towards an inclusive education system. Some are further along that road than others. The challenge is not to develop an inclusive system, but an effective one – one that caters for all and will help all children and young people reach their potential. Too often an inclusive policy means taking the middle ground and displaying a token acceptance to minority groups, which is often superficial and ineffective. There is little doubt that over the last decade much has been done to support students with dyslexia within the school system. But support does not necessarily equate with inclusion. A group or individual can be supported and still not feel fully included in the mainstream curriculum. Indeed in the case of dyslexia much of the effective support that has taken place has been in the form of specialised help and that has actually promoted the practice of exclusion rather than inclusion.

It is important in the case of children and young people with dyslexia that mainstream strategies are adapted and differentiated so that the students can benefit from mainstream classroom teaching as well as any specialist input that may be necessary. The focus of this book is therefore on mainstream strategies and on equipping students with dyslexia with the skills and support needed for full curriculum access. It is important that the specialist tag that has been attached to dyslexia for so long is less prominent and that the *differences* rather than the *deficits* are acknowledged. It is important that all teachers in all schools are able to accommodate these differences within their day-to-day teaching practice.

The purpose of this first chapter is to provide a context for dyslexia to aid understanding and to pave the way for the subsequent chapters which will focus on accommodating the needs of all students with dyslexia.

Dyslexia

'Dyslexia' is a term that can be surrounded by confusion and ambiguity. This can give rise to anxiety for teachers and parents. This is because students with dyslexia can display different types of profiles and this can be confusing for teachers who may see two dyslexic children but each has a different profile and different challenges. This emphasises the importance of obtaining a full and informed assessment of the students' needs. An excellent outline of identification of dyslexia for teachers can be found in the series of booklets *Supporting Pupils with Dyslexia in the Primary School* (2011) that can be downloaded free of charge from the Dyslexia Scotland website www.dyslexiascotland. org.uk.

Core difficulties

There are a number of core characteristics of dyslexia that are important for identification and assessment. These include the following:

Reading, writing and spelling difficulties

- These can be noted when the learner is progressing well in other areas and seems to have a good oral understanding.
- Often poor reading (decoding) contrasted with good comprehension can be an indicator of dyslexia.
- Difficulties in recognising and remembering sounds in words.
- When reading aloud substitution of words with words which have similar meanings.
- Difficulty with rhyming, remembering for example nursery rhymes and remembering the sequence of the rhyme.
- Difficulty with the sequence of the alphabet.
- Poor word attack skills – particularly with unknown words.
- Slow and hesitant reading often with little expression.
- Spelling difficulties.
- An inconsistent writing style and a slow writing speed and perhaps reluctance to write a lengthy piece of work.

Processing difficulties

- Poor short-term and working memory.
- Difficulty remembering lists of information, even short lists, or short instructions.
- Poor long-term memory/organisational difficulties
- Difficulty in displaying knowledge and understanding in written work.
- This can also include a difficulty in recalling a sequence of events and organising information.

Although the degree of dyslexia can differ, the indicators are usually fairly constant, but these can also depend on the age of the child. It is also possible to note some of the indicators of dyslexia before children attend school: that is before they start to learn to read.

It is important to recognise that dyslexia occurs within a continuum and that there can be shared and overlapping characteristics between dyslexia and other specific learning difficulties. For example some children with dyslexia can also display motor difficulties such as those associated with dyspraxia or have numbers problems as in dyscalculia.

It is important therefore to identify the actual characteristics of dyslexia. The notion of co-morbidity (referring to overlapping conditions, e.g. ADHD/dyslexia) can mean that the identification of the label is the starting point, not the end product. After the label is suspected it is important to probe further to identify the actual nature of the difficulties and the barriers preventing progress in learning.

Dyslexia is a term that is frequently used in schools and in the wider community – yet a term that many would admit is surrounded by some uncertainty. Such uncertainty does not help the teacher understand the needs of children with dyslexia and this can in fact give rise to anxiety. It is the aim of this book to clarify the confusion surrounding dyslexia from the class teachers' perspective and to highlight some strategies for identification and teaching. There will be a focus on a curriculum perspective in order to ensure that learners will have access to the full curriculum within an inclusive education environment.

Definitions

One of the areas of confusion centres on issues relating to definitions of dyslexia. There is a range of definitions that are currently used to describe dyslexia. Burden (2002) suggests that dyslexia is a 'convenience term' because it can embrace a number of different types of difficulties and, therefore, the term 'dyslexia' in itself is not helpful. While there is some validity in this – mainly because of the overlapping features between dyslexia and other types of difficulties – it is evading the issue to describe dyslexia as a 'convenience' term. It is important for the individual and for the parents to know if dyslexia is present and of course this can also be useful in the development of an individualised programme of learning.

There are some core characteristics of dyslexia that are important for identification and assessment and for the development of an Individual Educational Plan (IEP), and teaching and curriculum materials. These characteristics – whatever the term used to describe them – can present considerable barriers to learning for children and young people in school. It may be helpful to view dyslexia from the perspective of attempting to identify and address the barriers to literacy and learning that can be experienced by the child. These barriers may lie within the classroom environment as well as the nature of the learning task and cognitive challenges associated with learning. In order to address these, curriculum and task differentiation is essential as well as informed and detailed training of staff. The provision of specialised resources, which are available in abundance, is not the key to success. The key is informed understanding and this stems from effective training!

Policy and reports

There has been a significant impetus in many countries to develop policy on dyslexia. The practice and how policy is implemented is still very inconsistent – even within countries. One of the most groundbreaking government reports was from the Republic of Ireland (*Task Report on Dyslexia 2001*) followed by the Northern Ireland Government (*Task Group Report on Dyslexia 2002*), which also published extensive policy documents on dyslexia. Indeed in the Preface to the Northern Ireland task group report the Minister for Education indicated that the report highlighted a very real concern and one that provided challenges for all in education. This concern, he suggested, surrounds:

> *particularly the need for training for classroom teachers in recognising where children have, or may have, dyslexia and in putting in place the means to address their difficulties.*

Similarly, in England and Wales there have been vigorous dyslexia-friendly schools' campaigns that have been supported by the government in collaboration with the British Dyslexia Association. This has resulted in materials being widely circulated to schools and significant efforts to provide an education authority-wide attempt to identify and tackle dyslexia. Scotland has also witnessed collaboration between education authorities, the Scottish Executive, teacher education institutions and voluntary associations to develop assessment materials, teaching programmes, and resources for identification and intervention for dyslexia (Reid, 2001; Crombie, 2002, 2009; Reid et al., 2005).

In the Rose Report ('Identifying and teaching children and young people with dyslexia and literacy difficulties', 2009), the author suggests that 'The quality of an education system cannot exceed the quality of its teachers'. He goes on to say that this is an obvious truth, which applies to the assessment and teaching of learners of any age who are dyslexic. Success, the report suggests, depends first and foremost on teachers who know what they are doing and why they are doing it (pp. 15–16). This has considerable implications for teacher training and ensuring that there is a more widespread awareness of dyslexia throughout the school.

Professional involvement and perspectives

The diversity in research of dyslexia which is evident at the neurological, cognitive and educational levels (see Reid, 2009 and Everatt and Reid, 2009 for detailed discussion of this) has resulted in many professional and other groups being involved in developing different types of intervention. This can be confusing to both parents and teachers as often they may have to incorporate a range of different perspectives which may actually be conflicting. For example, the following professional groups can each have some input into a case conference on a child with dyslexia:

- Class teacher
- Educational adviser for the Education Authority
- Special Educational Needs Coordinator (SENCO)/learning support
- Educational psychologist
- Clinical psychologist
- Occupational therapist
- Information and Communication Technology (ICT) specialist
- Visual specialists
- Speech therapists, and of course
- Parents.

The different research perspectives that can account for the range of possible perspectives is noted in the British Psychological Society (BPS) working party report into assessment of dyslexia (BPS, 1999a). The report offers ten different hypotheses to explain and understand dyslexia. Some of these relate to cognitive aspects such as how children process information, some to reading characteristics such as phonological awareness and visual processing difficulties, and others to learning opportunities and environmental factors. This can provide some indication of the broad scope of dyslexia.

Research on dyslexia has developed considerably over the last 20 years. The advances in Magnetic Resonance Imaging (MRI) and other forms of brain imagery have been of great benefit to neuroscientists investigating factors relating to dyslexia. From these studies a number of different factors have emerged focusing on structural and functional brain-related factors. There is however little widespread agreement on the importance of the different aspects of dyslexia. Stein (2008) argues that there is genetic, sensory, motor and psychological evidence that dyslexia is a neurological syndrome affecting the development of the brain. He also provides evidence that the development of magnocellular neurones is impaired in children with dyslexia. Stein argues that the visual system provides the main input to the different routes for reading and therefore vision should be seen as the most important sense for reading. This view however is strongly disputed by many because they believe that acquisition of phonological skills is in fact much more crucial for successful reading (Vellutino *et al.*, 2004).

Additionally Fawcett and Nicolson (2008) argue there is now extensive evidence that the cerebellum is implicated with difficulties in a range of motor, language and cognitive activities. Fawcett and Nicolson (2008) argue that the cerebellar deficit hypothesis may provide close to a single coherent explanation of the three of the key criteria relating to dyslexia – reading, writing and spelling.

Cognitive research

Cognitive research looks at processing factors: memory, processing speed and effectiveness of learning. These are areas of considerable importance and according to Everatt and Reid (2009) may be considered as the most likely to link research with classroom practices.

The dominant causal viewpoint on the factors associated with dyslexia however is the phonological deficit hypothesis. This perspective has been derived from substantial evidence that difficulties in phonological processing, particularly when related to phonological decoding, have been a major distinguishing factor between dyslexics and non-dyslexics. Children who find it difficult to distinguish sounds within verbally presented words would be predicted to have problems learning the alphabetic principle that letters represent sounds. It is argued that it is this population of children who are more likely to develop dyslexia.

Implications for teaching

The research does have implications for teaching and supporting children within an inclusive education environment. This is discussed in some detail by Norwich and Lewis (2005), who propose the view that teaching approaches themselves should be seen as on a continuum and children with dyslexia do not need anything different, or special, but can be placed at a different point in the continuum. This would imply that the pedagogy and the curriculum are the same for all, although there may be a greater degree of adaptation in some cases. Taking the Norwich and Lewis view one step further one can note that the key aspect relates to supporting students with dyslexia in the mainstream and ensuring that all teachers, and not a few specialists, have a sound understanding of what actually constitutes dyslexia and how it can be evident in classroom work.

However, the Norwich and Lewis view is controversial as many of the specialised approaches that have been developed for children with dyslexia rely to a great extent on the opportunity to pull the child out of class and implement approaches on a one-on-one basis (Reid 2009). This dilemma between specialism and general approaches however can be overcome according to Coffield *et al.* (2008), who suggest that the development of 'dyslexia-friendly standards' for all schools within a local authority can provide a useful tool for developing effective class intervention for students with dyslexia.

As Houston (2011) points out, 'it is a teacher's responsibility to provide a suitably differentiated curriculum, accessible to all children, that provides each with the opportunity to develop and apply individual strengths. Responsibilities for meeting the additional needs of children with dyslexia are the same as those for all children, and should include approaches that avoid unnecessary dependence on written text'. She goes on to indicate that while dyslexia is not linked to ability, able children with dyslexia may persistently underachieve in relation to their academic potential. This is an important point as it is too easy to let students with dyslexia drift along if they are coping okay with the work of the class; but as Houston points out, they may well be underachieving. Houston also adds that there needs to be an acceptance that some children with dyslexia may require additional support and that consultation between colleagues and specialists is necessary to determine how best to provide this.

Hidden disability

There is however some agreement that dyslexia represents more than a reading difficulty. While there are many well-enunciated principles for teaching children with dyslexia, a closer examination of these indicate that many of these principles incorporate good teaching practices which will in fact benefit all children.

Dyslexia can be described as a hidden disability because we may not know the person has dyslexia until they are put into a situation that requires skills in literacy or processing certain types of information. At school many children become skilled at covering up and compensating for their dyslexic difficulties, usually by avoiding reading aloud or writing as little as possible. Sometimes dyslexia can be misunderstood for laziness or lack of interest in school work. In reality that is far from the case – usually children with dyslexia extend more effort than others because of their difficulty, and may often become tired very easily as a result of this effort.

This aspect of a hidden disability can often result in the child being misunderstood. Jamie Oliver, the celebrity chef, describing his own schooling in the UK said: 'It was with great regret that I didn't do better at school. People just thought I was thick. It was a struggle, I never really had anyone to help that understood dyslexia and who could bring out my strengths' (http://dyslexicadvantage.com/photo/entrepreneurs-with-dyslexia?context=user accessed 14 August 2011). Indeed the Dyslexia Advantage website http://dyslexicadvantage.com/page/dyslexics-on-dyslexia has a host of illuminating stories from successful dyslexic people – as wide-ranging as children's authors, architects, lawyers and medical doctors. A book published in association with Dyslexia Scotland – *Dyslexia and Us: a collection of personal stories* – also describes how many people have overcome adversity and faced with this hidden disability sought out promising and successful careers. Sir Jackie Stewart in the foreword to the book emphasises the key point that today dyslexia is talked about more openly than it ever has been. This is of fundamental importance as it promotes dialogue which leads to understanding. The hidden disability aspect can also come from the students themselves. Many try (quite understandably) to hide their difficulties and this can make identification and support more difficult to achieve. One student from the book *Dyslexia and Us* remarks 'when I was in primary school I knew I was different from the other students, but I didn't know why, so I hid it from everybody'. This type of situation can be very common and is one that all teachers must be aware of so that children will not need to hide and feel ashamed of their difficulties.

Programmes and resources

It is important therefore to ensure that class teachers have an understanding of dyslexia and of the strategies and supports that are appropriate and can be readily applied to the classroom without necessarily referring to costly commercially produced materials.

There is of course a wide range of programmes and resources which have been specifically developed for use for children with dyslexia. Many of these are excellent and will be referred to later in this book. But many of the approaches that can be considered *dyslexia appropriate* can be developed by the class teacher. Consider the list below. This is a checklist of dyslexia-appropriate practices and these do not necessarily mean that expensive resources need to be used. Yet by adhering to this list the student with dyslexia may be able to access texts and deal with tasks that may otherwise have been out of reach.

Table 1.1 Worksheet checklist

Worksheet checklist	Yes/No
Have small steps been used?	
Are the sentences short?	
Is the vocabulary easy to understand?	
Have visuals been used?	
Has large print been used?	
Is the font style appropriate?	
Has enough attention been given to presentation?	
Are there opportunities for self-monitoring and self-correction?	
Are the tasks within the child's comfort zone?	
Is there a variety of different types of tasks?	
Are there opportunities for group work as well as individual work?	

Source: Reid and Green (2011).

Characteristics of dyslexia

Auditory aspects

Auditory processing is an important element in developing language and reading skills. The development of phonological awareness relies on this and phonological awareness is seen as a crucial factor in dyslexia. Phonological awareness relates to the differentiating of sounds, especially sounds that are similar, remembering these sounds and identifying them in words. These aspects can present difficulties for dyslexic children.

Visual processing

Some children with dyslexia can have some visual disturbance when reading print and this can cause blurring, words merging and omissions of words or lines when reading. Coloured overlays for some children have been successful, as has the use of coloured background for text and the font characteristics and font size. It has suggested that visual filters (coloured lenses that are worn, or coloured overlays that are placed over the page, when reading) may be effective for alleviating (at least some) reading difficulties (Irlen, 1991; Wilkins, 2004).

Neurological connections

The connections between the different parts of the brain are crucial for effective learning. It is these connections that help with the integration of different skills such as visual/ motor integration, as in copying, and auditory/kinaesthetic integration as in listening and carrying out instructions and in combining the visual and auditory stimuli when reading. There is considerable research evidence that highlights the neurological basis of dyslexia and in particular the connecting pathways of the left and right hemispheres as well as aspects relating to the cerebellum and the magnoceller visual system (see Breznitz (2008), Everatt (2002) and Fawcett and Nicolson (2008)). These factors affect processing speed (Breznitz (2008) as well as visual accuracy (Everatt 2002) and motor co-ordination (Portwood (1999), Fawcett and Nicolson (2008)).

The core difficulties – educational performance

The core difficulties associated with dyslexia are reading, spelling and writing. These tasks are usually left-hemisphere skills, apart from creative writing, which can be associated with the right hemisphere. The research indicates that children with dyslexia can have weaknesses in the left hemisphere, so therefore tasks involving phonics, accuracy, sequencing and remembering will be more challenging and often more exhausting for the child with dyslexia.

Some of the difficulties that are experienced include:

Reading

- Difficulty in recognising sounds in words.

- Difficulty in remembering the combinations of letters that make up sounds such as 'ph' and 'th' and remembering these and using them in a word.
- Sequencing the sounds and the letters in words in the correct order.
- Substitution of words when reading aloud, for example saying 'car' for 'bus'.
- Difficulty with rhyming, remembering, for example nursery rhymes and remembering the sequence of the rhyme.
- Possible difficulty sounding out sounds in words.
- Reversing, omitting or adding letters.
- Losing the place when reading.
- Difficulty with the sequence of the alphabet.
- Difficulty pronouncing multi-syllabic words, even common ones.
- Poor word attack skills: particularly with unknown words.
- Slow and hesitant reading, often with little expression.
- Reluctance to read for pleasure.
- Reading comprehension tends to be better than single-word reading.
- Confusing words which have the same or similar sounds – such as 'their' and 'there' and 'access' and 'assess'.

Spelling

- Difficulty remembering spelling rules.
- Making phonological errors in spelling, for example 'f' for 'ph'.
- Letters out of sequence.
- Inconsistent use of some letters with similar sounds such as 's' and 'z'.
- Difficulty with word endings for example using 'ie' for 'y'.
- Confusion or omission of vowels.
- Difficulty with words with double consonants such as 'commission'.

Writing

- Inconsistent writing style.
- Slow writing speed.
- Inconsistent use of capital and small letters.
- Reluctance to write any lengthy piece.
- Sometimes an unusual writing grip or sitting position.

The role of the environment

The role and the impact of the environment on a student with dyslexia are considerable. The classroom design as well as the school layout is worth noting. Some classroom environments may be more suited to left-hemisphere learners, while others to right-hemisphere. Left-hemisphere learners generally prefer a quiet, formal and predictable environment, while right-hemisphere learners prefer a more random, informal and usually visually and auditory stimulating environment. The research seems to indicate that students with dyslexia lean more towards right-hemisphere processing (West, 2009).

Some key factors in the learning environment that are important for learners with dyslexia are:

Layout

The organization of classroom furniture is an important consideration. If possible ensure a range of options for work bases, including individual desks with a degree of seclusion and open work spaces that can facilitate group work. Students with dyslexia will need both.

There are many different ways of arranging learners' desks. Rows and squares are two of the most popular. It is a good idea to provide an alternative as different tasks may require a different type of layout. Flexibility therefore is important and being able to move and adjust the layout of the classroom should be considered. There is nothing quite as frustrating as having classroom furniture fixed – for example when the desks are fixed to the chairs or they are fixed to the floor. Ideally the type of the classroom furniture should offer some flexibility so that it can be moved and rearranged. Flexibility is the key for students with dyslexia.

Predictability and routine

Most children and particularly children with dyslexia can often obtain security from routine. It is therefore necessary to introduce some routine and sameness into the classroom environment. But at the same time children often become more stimulated by the unexpected and can become quite excited with change. But this should be carefully introduced and monitored.

Structure

Children with dyslexia benefit a great deal from structure, but at the same time it is important not to over-structure the environment. One of the key aims of education is to promote independent thinking – and this applies to children with dyslexia. This may be restricted if the learning environment is over-structured. A classroom environment that is too structured can very easily become teacher-centred. It is important to turn this into a learner-centred environment so the structure would have some flexibility to accommodate the needs of the learner with dyslexia.

Visual appeal

The effect of a classroom environment can make an impact almost as soon as one enters a classroom. This first impression is very important and can often be determined by the visual appeal of the classroom. This is important for the children with dyslexia as they can be visual learners (West, 2009) but also for parents as it can be very welcoming.

Ownership and responsibility

It is crucial that children with dyslexia feel they have some control over the learning space. This is an important factor in promoting learner independence and is particularly important for students with dyslexia as it is too easy for them to become dependent on a teacher or a learning support teacher. Giving them some control over their environment can also help to give them responsibility for their own learning.

Stimulate all the senses

It is now well established that learning is more effective for learners with dyslexia if it is multisensory. That means the learning environment should accommodate visual, auditory and kinaesthetic learning preferences. This can be done through making available wall displays, tapes and headphones, and facilitating the freedom to move around the classroom and to explore different learning situations.

Stress-free

A crucial factor irrespective of the type of classroom environment is that it is free from stress. Children with dyslexia can be very sensitive to stress in the learning situation – many find learning stressful, so it is important that the environment is as stress-free as possible. Music can help in this respect but the general ambiance and ethos can be tailored towards a stress-free environment.

Allow scope for social interaction

This is important for children with dyslexia. They often learn more effectively through groupwork, so space is an important consideration when planning activities. It is important to spend some time planning the composition of groups and taking the students learning styles into consideration. It is a good idea to have a mix of styles in a group so that the student with dyslexia does not feel too different from anyone else. It is crucial therefore that the school is seen as a welcoming and positive learning environment

The role of the label

Usually the term 'dyslexia' is only applied after a fairly extensive assessment process as it is important that labels are not unnecessarily applied. A label usually brings a set of expectations. These can relate to a more informed selection of resources or a different set of expectations from parents and perhaps teachers. While a label can be helpful, it can also be disadvantageous and may lead to a resignation that dyslexia can only be dealt with by 'experts'. This is a misguided assumption, and may lead teachers to feel they possess neither the skills nor the training to deal with dyslexia in the classroom. Yet in fact there is no specific approach that is universally recognised to manage dyslexia. The notion of multi-sensory approaches involving the use of visual, auditory, kinesthetic and tactile strategies are believed to be essential for children with dyslexia, yet such approaches are also useful for all children and indeed incorporate elements of good teaching. There are, however, many specific teaching programmes often used with children with dyslexia that are built around these approaches. It is also important that teachers have an enhanced understanding of the type of difficulties experienced by children with dyslexia.

The key point, therefore, in teaching children with dyslexia is knowledge of good teaching practices, not access to resources. It is important that the teacher has knowledge and understanding of the type of difficulties associated with dyslexia and also of the actual child, i.e. his or her profile, background, difficulties, strengths and the strategies that have already been utilized. This is extremely important as the profile of strengths and difficulties presented by children with dyslexia can differ. This, therefore, means that the responsibility for teaching children with dyslexia lies not with a 'specialist', but with class teachers who have the knowledge and the experience of adapting and differentiating teaching materials, and are able to adapt their teaching to suit the needs of the learner. Aspects relating to curriculum development are also crucial and the needs of children with dyslexia can be met, as much through careful planning of curriculum and teaching objectives, as through the use of specialised materials.

Dyslexia as a difference

Dyslexia can be described as a **difference** in the way some people process information. This means that reading accurately, and at speed, can be difficult for children with dyslexia, as can spelling accurately and writing in a structured manner. The individual with dyslexia can become confused when several instructions are given at the same time, and will usually have poor short-term memory, difficulty with directional orientation, such as telling right from left and map reading. They may also have a word-finding difficulty and in discussions and conversation may use inappropriate words – perhaps confusing words that sound or look similar – such as 'were'/'where' and 'there'/'their'. They may also confuse syllables in words, or put these in the wrong order when writing or talking, such as 'preliminary' or 'elephant'. For example, for 'preliminary' they may read or say 'preinlimary'. But essentially the characteristics can amount to a different way of processing information – they usually have a visual, right-brained global processing style but it is important to acknowledge the strengths in this style, as well as considering the difficulties.

Summary

It is important that our understanding of dyslexia – particularly within the inclusive learning situation – accommodates to factors relating to the learning process. This can have implications for how the child with dyslexia functions in the classroom. It is also important that all staff in a school have an adequate and appropriate understanding of what dyslexia is. It is important that they do not only see it as a specialist area for which they have little or no responsibility. In order to meet the needs of all students with dyslexia it is important for training to be provided on a whole school basis and the responsibility for dealing with dyslexia is a shared responsibility. While it is important to acknowledge that many children with dyslexia will require a specialist programme, some others may perform well with the approaches advocated in the now well-established dyslexia friendly guidance (see British Dyslexia Association (BDA) website). This implies that the responsibility is on the school and indeed the education authority to ensure that awareness is present, support is available and that all teachers are trained.

2 Inclusion: issues and challenges

This chapter discusses the following:

- Definitions of inclusion
- Key principles of inclusion
- Government initiatives
- Issues and challenges.

The term 'inclusion' implies that the needs of all students should be met within the mainstream school. This however presents quite a dilemma in relation to providing for all students and at the same time acknowledging the 'diversity' that is present in all school populations. The desire to obtain full inclusion can result in considerable challenges particularly if it is brought about too hastily. It is important to train all staff in understanding the diverse needs of their students. If it happens too quickly any training that has taken place will not have had sufficient time to make an impact on staff. This is particularly the situation in relation to dyslexia as there may be some misguided beliefs on what constitutes dyslexia and particularly the range of characteristics associated with dyslexia and the best type of intervention. For that reason it is preferable to see inclusion as a process that takes place over time.

Artemi Sakellariadis (2012), Director of the Centre for Studies on Inclusive Education (CSIE) in the UK suggests that developing inclusive provision is not so much about what you do, as about how you do it. She asserts that 'we are talking about a process, not a method'. This means that developing an inclusive system of provision will take place over time and cannot happen overnight.

Whilst 'inclusion' may mean that the needs of all children should be met within the mainstream school, it is important to appreciate that it does not necessarily mean that the student must be in the mainstream classroom all the time. The CSIE states in its inclusion charter that:

> Time spent out of the ordinary classroom for appropriate individual or group work on a part-time basis is not segregation. Neither is removal for therapy or because of disruption, provided it is time-limited, for a specified purpose ... Any time-out from the ordinary classroom should not affect a student's right to full membership of the mainstream (Thomas and Vaughn, 2004, p. 137).

There are also other views that reject inclusion as necessarily being about location, placement or presence. Baroness Mary Warnock, for example, has rejected educational inclusion as 'all children under the same roof'. She prefers a common curriculum concept of inclusion:

> including all children in the common educational enterprise of learning, wherever they learn best (Warnock, 2005, p. 14).

The definition of 'inclusion' developed by Reid (2011) is as follows:

> *Inclusion is a **process** that accommodates to the educational, social and emotional needs of children, young people and families. Inclusion is **not** synonymous with mainstream schooling. The inclusive process can incorporate a range of special-ised provision that can be accessed, according to need. A key factor that deter-mines the success or otherwise, of inclusive provision is the training of staff, and the impact of that training in the planning, differentiation and presentation of the curriculum. At the same time full management commitment needs to be present* (Reid 2011).

Important aspects of this definition are the impact of the training and the commitment of management. There could be a considerable amount of good intentions among staff at school, but without management support and adequate training those good intentions can easily disappear. Management must be seen as being committed to ensuring that all the staff are prepared for the diversity of students in an inclusive school. To do this they need an understanding of special needs and dyslexia. Dealing with children with any type of special need for teachers who are unaccustomed to this can be a daunting prospect.

Norwich (2009) on the other hand sees inclusion as a 'flexible interacting continua of provision'. He also cites Mary Warnock to support his viewpoint in her suggestion that educational inclusion should be seen as a curriculum concept (including all children in the common educational enterprise of learning, wherever they learn best (Warnock, 2005, p. 14)).

There are a number of different definitions of inclusion and much depends on the perspective taken – some view inclusion from a social perspective, while others may take a purely educational viewpoint. The following statement by Tony Booth indicates a mix of both of these, though it is slanted towards the educational point of view. '[Inclusion is] participation in the cultures, curricula and communities of *local* schools' (*Inclusion Index*, Booth *et al.*, 2000).

Those views have important implications for students with dyslexia as they often do require specialist support. There are many examples of this in the USA, Canada and the UK. This can be in the form of small-scale unit provision, separate schools or one-on-one withdrawal within the mainstream school. The British Dyslexia Association highlight different forms of provision in their annual handbook (BDA 2011). In this publication they place provision for students with dyslexia into categories depending on the extent of staff training, specialisation and support available.

Mittler (2001) argues that schools need to rethink their values. This means they need to restructure their organisation, curriculum and assessment arrangements in order to help diverse groups of students overcome barriers to learning and participation in the full curriculum.

The question that arises however is how compatible is dyslexia with inclusive education. Much of the success of inclusive provision rests on the 'readiness to include' and this depends on the level of training and how prepared teachers and schools are for these challenges. In order for children with dyslexia to have their needs fully met in mainstream school there is a need for all teachers to be at least familiar with dyslexia and also the wider range of special educational needs as there is often an overlap between different types of conditions. There is also a trend for de-specialising dyslexia. The implication is that all class teachers should have an awareness and skills in dealing with dyslexia and other specific needs. Those teachers who have specialist training and experience can certainly play a vitally important role in this process. They can pass on their skills to class teachers and help to ensure that all staff have an awareness and some training in areas such as dyslexia, but it is also important to recognise the expertise and experience that specialist practitioners have built up over the years (Bell and McLean, 2012).

Class teachers are under considerable pressure. Continuous and formative assessment, the development of IEPs, early intervention initiatives and curriculum planning can exert considerable time pressures on teachers. Some dyslexic children also require a high degree of individual support and this can put added pressure on teachers. Classroom teachers are seeking training and access to the resources that can help meet the needs of dyslexic children. This has now been acknowledged by the UK and other governments as a priority (see Rose, 2009).

The idea that inclusion is a process implies that inclusion should be seen in its broadest sense, utilising the support of community resources as well as collaboration with parents. Full inclusion can only become a reality if the whole community is included. This means that links with community facilities such as libraries, community centres and organisations such as housing associations and co-operatives that may not be directly involved in education are essential, as inclusion is not only about full access to education but about social fairness and equitable distribution of resources.

Norwich (2009) argues that the continuum idea arises from the idea that there is a range of options along each dimension of need. He suggests that provision is planned to meet individual needs and requirements in the form of high levels of commonality and low levels of differentiation or low levels of commonality and high levels of differentiation, as appropriate. Norwich refers to this as flexible interacting continua of provision. This provision could include separate schooling (possibly a special school linked to an ordinary school), same class with varying degrees of withdrawal, or same learning group. There is certainly much to commend in Norwich's approach because children with dyslexia do not readily fit into one or the other, for example some may need a high level of commonality, while other may need a high level of differentiation.

Riddell, Weedon and Harris (2012) suggest that there is a dilemma between universalism (treating all the same) and the concept of 'difference', but there continues to be a commitment to the over-arching categories of Special Educational Needs (SEN) and Additional Support Needs. They also argue that there are moves towards the use of fine-grained categories, suggesting a focus on pupil differences and that some of these categories have gained currency as a result of pressure from parents and voluntary organizations (e.g. autistic spectrum disorder and dyslexia), or as a result of professional pressures. With this view we enter the arena of political debate, understandable given the impact of government influence in education certainly since the 1970s. The field of dyslexia is no stranger to political manoeuvrings.

This body of work in relation to the influences and the impact of inclusion is reflected in an 'organizational paradigm' of research in SEN (Skidmore, 2004). Having been influenced by the school effectiveness tradition, David Skidmore argues that researchers saw special needs as arising from deficiencies in the way schools were organized and this led to moves to attempt to restructure schools. Whole school training and school systems then became a focus of intervention for educational psychologists and educationists (e.g. McLean (2008), *The Motivated School*).

Social and medical models

Avramidis and Norwich (2012) suggest that the last 30 years has witnessed a move from a medical (individual) model to a more social model and that this model views disability as socially created. They argue that the significance of the origins of the social model is that it underpinned the development of ideas about inclusive education. This and the thrust towards the 'organizational paradigm' of research in SEN (Skidmore, 2004) have shifted the focus from individuals' needs to school systems. They suggest that the school effectiveness tradition saw special needs as resulting from deficiencies in the way schools were organized and this led to projects and initiatives on school restructuring. As a result of this it has been suggested that inclusion has advanced on the basis of socio-political arguments rather than empirical evidence and individual needs (Farrell, 2001; Lindsay, 2003). At the school level this requires curriculum planning and shared objectives between home and school. Consultation and planning appear to be two of the key factors that can bring about such equity and consequently full access to the curriculum.

Norwich (2009) argues that the social model is associated with assumptions that disabled people are disabled by prejudice and discrimination, not by their impairments. Riddick (2001) applies these ideas to dyslexia by suggesting that the phonological impairment associated with dyslexia can lead to a disability 'because of society and particularly schools' attitudes to literacy' (Riddick, 2001, p. 226).

According to Norwich (2009) inclusion relates to different dimensions, for example, levels in the system (national, school, class); placement (separate to general settings); participation (academic–social); and curriculum (common–different content). Norwich therefore proposes that inclusion should be seen in terms of multiple dimensions of provision, '***flexible interacting continua of provision***', where there are various options which reflect varying balances between common and differentiated aspects.

Challenges

There are a number of challenges that are evident in relation to inclusion for students with dyslexia. Giorcelli (1999) suggests that the controversy surrounding inclusion is due to the lack of preparedness of teachers in mainstream schools for students such as those with dyslexia. This issue has been given a high priority, with groups advocating for effective inclusion, such as the Academy for Inclusion of Special Needs (see www.globaleducationalconsultants.com/projects.html), which runs fully accredited courses on teaching in relation to a range of learning needs taking the principles and practices of inclusion into account.

Wearmouth, Soler and Reid (2002) suggest that the current educational context is one that attempts to reconcile the principles of individuality, distinctiveness and diversity with inclusion and equal opportunities and in this there are inherent conflicts. On the one hand while inclusion can be seen as a desirable outcome in terms of equity, it can also be seen as a threat and a potential conflict between meeting the needs of individuals and meeting the needs of all.

Although they were referring to all learners, the view from Simpson and Ure (1993) can also describe good practices that can be used to help meet the needs of children with dyslexia. The most effective teachers in their study displayed the following:

- Sharing the management of learning with pupils.
- Promoting the belief that things can improve by demonstrating that agreed learning strategies work.
- Using a wide range of sources of information.
- Giving and receiving continuous feedback in terms of how pupils are getting on.

These statements confirmed the need to incorporate student's perspectives into the practical development of inclusive practices. Each of these statements can also be consistent with the needs of children with dyslexia.

The General Statement on Inclusion in the UK (QCA 2000) on 'providing effective learning opportunities for all pupils' sets out three 'key principles for inclusion':

- Setting suitable learning challenges.
- Responding to pupils' diverse learning needs.
- Overcoming potential barriers to learning and assessment for individuals and groups of pupils.

It is important that these statements are considered for students with dyslexia as they need learning challenges – too often this is neglected in the desire to remediate their weaknesses in literacy. Students with dyslexia can also show diverse characteristics. It is important to also recognise within-group diversity and to identify the barriers and potential barriers to learning, thus advocating a proactive approach to dealing with dyslexia.

Some key points on inclusion

- Inclusion does not just happen – it is a process.
- School culture and within-school and community collaboration are essential for inclusion.
- Inclusion can highlight a potential conflict between meeting the needs of individuals and meeting the needs of all.
- Norwich's flexible interacting continua of provision can provide an effective way to deal with these conflicts.

Student perspectives

It is important to consider parent and student perspectives when focusing on how inclusion can benefit students with dyslexia. Wearmouth (2001) suggests that one of the major challenges is engaging with student perspectives in a positive and meaningful way. This means that self-advocacy is an important consideration when developing inclusive provision. Garner and Sandow (1995) suggest there are philosophical and practical problems surrounding pupil self-advocacy that can be uncomfortable for teachers. Self-advocacy they suggest may run contrary to the traditional behaviourist model of learning adopted in some schools in which students have clearly defined roles and expectations. Additionally, some may see students as not fully capable of contributing rationally to decisions about their own lives. Self-advocacy involves a transfer of power from teacher to student and for many this may be too big a risk to take. It is therefore heartening to see self-advocacy given a prominent position in the information booklet of a school that specialises in dyslexia. The school handbook for the Lighthouse School in Cairo (www.lighthouseschoolonline.com) indicates that social values such as respect, responsibility, cooperation and self-advocacy are important vehicles in helping our students compensate for their learning challenges. Many other schools with specialised provision in the UK, the USA and Canada have similarly recognised the need to promote self-advocacy. For example the Kenneth Gordon School in Vancouver, BC comment that 'self-disclosure is an important factor if students are to develop a healthy perception of their dyslexia and the associated challenges. It is also important for achieving self-advocacy' (http://www.kgms.ca).

Self-advocacy does assume that there will be an identification and recognition of the needs of students with dyslexia. For students further up the school at college or university this may mean self-disclosure. But to be able to self-disclose and be a self-advocate the student has to have some understanding of dyslexia and what it means to them. This should commence as early as possible in the student's schooling. Yet often self-disclosure can present dilemmas for students with dyslexia. Pryce and Gerber (2007) provide some insights into self-disclosure. These are summarised below.

1. Self-disclosure is driven by context and situation.
    It is important that dyslexia is disclosed at the right time and in the right place.
2. Self-disclosure is the management of personal information.
    All information pertaining to disability is private and confidential. Whether all or part of that information is shared, and how it is shared, is at the discretion of the person with the (learning) disability.
3. Self-disclosure is nestled in the larger concept of self-determination.
    Disclosure is just one part of self-determination that empowers persons with learning disabilities to have control over the choice of disclosure.
4. There is risk to self-disclosure.
    There are no guarantees in disclosure. It can be a plus but it can be a negative when disclosure produces misunderstanding, stigma or bias.
5. Disclosure must include information and not just the label.
    The term 'learning disabilities' or even 'dyslexia' lacks specificity and even has different meanings in different countries such as the United States and UK. It is helpful if disclosure is accompanied by the challenges the adults face and the accommodations that are necessary.
6. Disclosure is just the beginning.
    When the decision to disclose is made, it is important to consider that it is the beginning of a dynamic process that will necessitate self-advocacy skills.

Self-disclosure can also be influenced by the need for the student to be accepted and 'fit in' to the student group. This can be made more challenging when the student has perceptions of his or her dyslexia as a disability. Young and Browning (2004) maintain that self-advocacy skills are among the most critical skills necessary for the adult in systems of all kinds, whether education, training, employment or financial assistance. These skills however need to be developed at school. They support the notion of using the disability model as they suggest the use of this model helps to 'shift the power relationships' between the person with learning disabilities/dyslexia and programmes and work. For example, if an individual comes into the workplace and says, 'I learn differently', the employer is not legally required to provide any kind of accommodation.

On the other hand the individual coming in saying 'I have a disability' creates a situation requiring the employer to provide reasonable accommodations that would allow the employee with a disability to perform their job and to compete on a level playing field. This is an interesting perspective and although it is taken from the workplace context it does have application for school. David McLoughlin (McLoughlin, 2002) from the Adult Dyslexia and Skills Development Centre in London, however, suggests that if dyslexic people are to be fully *included* in society the emphasis should be on empowerment or enablement rather than a model of disability that perceives the 'dyslexic as a victim'. He suggests that empowerment comes from self-understanding and understanding by others. Self-understanding is crucial and for that reason it is important that school-age students with dyslexia have a clear understanding of how dyslexia affects their learning.

Cooper (2009) provides an interesting insight into what it is like to be dyslexic which can be summed up in the comment 'take away the dyslexia and it would no longer be me'. The implication of this is that the identity of being dyslexic is important and that dyslexia for many is a way of life – it is *them* and they need others to appreciate that and not try to make them 'better'. Support and empathy is the answer and along with this goes the need to help the dyslexic person develop self-advocacy skills. Helping students with dyslexia to become aware of how they learn and giving them this self-knowledge can be beneficial for developing self-advocacy and self-esteem, students should therefore be given:

- An understanding of dyslexia: what it is and how it affects them.
- Knowledge of their own learning style, which will enable them to use it when working on their own and can facilitate independent learning.
- The confidence and experience of being their own advocate as early in the education process as possible.

Parent perspectives

Many schools are now promoting more open-door policies and welcoming parents more and more into the school. This is essential as parents need to feel some form of ownership over the educational provision. This helps to promote trust that is essential when considering the best options for students with dyslexia.

TeacherNet suggest many ways that schools and parents can liaise, including more participation in school management, though they recognise that increased parental involvement in school management won't happen overnight. Initiatives such as this do represent a significant change in culture and behaviour for both parents and schools and this type of initiative will benefit all including parents, children and families as well as the school and the wider community.

In Australia the booklet '*Helping People with Dyslexia: A National Action Agenda*' (Bond *et al.*, 2010) highlights the need to communicate with parents and families. In the booklet, recommendation 12 advocates the need for an information booklet for families and carers that explains what new provisions for dyslexic children have been introduced and the role of parents.

Riddell, Weedon and Harris (2011) suggest that the balance of power between parents and professionals can result in positive and negative outcomes. They argue that on the one hand, individual parents may think that they are in the best position to determine their child's needs and appropriate provision, but on the other hand, local authorities may argue that they should retain the ultimate power in decision-making since they can act as impartial arbiters in the allocation of scare resources. This dilemma is not going to disappear but it does reinforce the need for dialogue and discussion, which of course was one of the aims of the parent partnerships developed in the UK in the Education Act 2001.

Yet Riddell *et al.* (2012) argue that in the field of special and additional support needs, along with many other spheres of education, parental power has traditionally been limited, with the local authority and professionals retaining control over resource allocation decisions. This is despite the establishment of a number of dispute-resolution mechanisms (since 1993 in England and 2004 in Scotland) that were intended to increase opportunities for parents to challenge local authority decisions. The research conducted by Riddell *et al.* on dispute resolution in special and additional support needs explored the use and perceptions of different ways of resolving disagreements (tribunal mediation and, in Scotland only, adjudication), and the results of the research question whether these mechanisms have succeeded in altering the balance of power between parents and local authorities. They do indicate however that the Parent Partnership Service (PPS) played a significant role in informal mediation. It was when this informal mediation failed that parents tended to opt for the tribunal rather than trying formal mediation. Formal mediation would involve requesting that the education authority address the issue and this usually involves a formal process.

Communication

This is the key to dealing with potential and actual conflicts that may occur. It is essential to establish communication with everyone working with the student as well as the parents or guardians. A strong learning team which communicates and provides regular feedback will aid in the student's success at school and at home. Following are some ideas that will help in maintaining a strong communication triangle between home, teacher and teaching assistant (communication with other learning support people who work with the student may be necessary and should also be encouraged).

- Establish a common goal.
- Create a team.
- Build bridges between school and home.
- Ask for regular feedback from students, teacher and parents/guardians.
- Use a notebook between home and school to keep a log and encourage communication.
- Use email to discuss any issues that may arise and include everyone on the child's learning team.
- Schedule regular meetings to discuss progress, goals, IEP, strategies, learning style, behaviour.
- Ensure that parents have confidence in the school by actively pursuing dyslexia-friendly policies and practices.

A number of issues and challenges have been noted in this chapter in relation to the dilemmas and the practices of meeting the needs of students with dyslexia within an inclusive provision. The last point – that of communication – is perhaps the most vital. It is through effective and positive communication that the needs of all can be met – children, parents and teachers.

3 Inclusion: responding to the challenge

The problem with labels

There is no doubt that labels can be very helpful and can be beneficial to students and parents as well as the teachers. They can provide a centre focus for the teacher and help with the main task of identifying the specific needs of the student and accommodating these needs within the curriculum. The changing social and historical context of education however has meant that a common national framework for education of most children has been developed and is centrally controlled. This applies to literacy and numeracy in particular and often government policies on these aspects take a midline approach and may not accommodate these children who need specialised approaches.

This can place classroom teachers in a position of some anxiety when they are faced with students whose needs are not readily met in the mainstream curriculum. Continuous assessment, the development of IEPs and curriculum planning can exert considerable time pressures on teachers. Very often children with dyslexia require a degree of individual support and this can put added pressure onto teachers. It is possible however for classroom teachers to utilise the resources and help of others in the school to ensure the needs of dyslexic children are met. For example, a sound working knowledge of the technology and support materials and how these can be used will be of enormous benefit when it comes to utilising all the support available (see Table 3.1 below), and in many classrooms teaching assistants are available. Teaching assistants can have a key role to play in this process but again training can be an issue (Reid and Green, 2008). There are also many studies showing the advantages and the potential of using parent helpers and in working co-operatively with the home as well as using senior pupils with younger students in peer tutoring programmes (Topping, 2002).

Table 3.1 ICT and dyslexia

Text help
The program known as TextHelp© is particularly useful for assisting with essay writing. Text help has a readback facility and has a spellchecker that includes a dyslexic spellcheck option that searches for common dyslexic errors. Additionally TextHelp© has a word prediction feature that can predict a word from the context of the sentence, giving up to ten options from a dropdown menu. Often dyslexic students have a word-finding difficulty and this feature can therefore be very useful. This software also has a 'word wizard' that provides the user with a definition of any word, options regarding homophones, an outline of a phonic map and a talking help file.

Inspiration
Inspiration is a software program that can help in the development of ideas and in the organisation of thinking. Through the use of diagrams it helps the student comprehend concepts and information. Essentially the use of diagrams can help to

make creating and modifying concept maps and ideas easier. The user can also prioritise and rearrange ideas, helping with essay writing. Inspiration can therefore be used for brainstorming, organizing, pre-writing, concept mapping, planning and outlining. There are 35 inbuilt templates and these can be used for a range of subjects including English, History and Science. Dyslexic learners often think in pictures rather than words. This technique can be used for note-taking, for remembering information and organizing ideas for written work. The Inspiration program converts an image into a linear outline.

www.r-e-m.co.uk has a comprehensive catalogue of software for use with children with dyslexia. Programs include: Starspell, Wordshark 3, Clicker 4 (which enables students to write with whole words and pictures), textHELP® read and write, Penfriend (which is able to predict words before they are typed), Wordswork (which uses a learning styles approach), Inspiration (for creative planning and brainstorming), Numbershark, Times Tables and Parenting Snakes and Ladders.

iANSYST Ltd – provides computers and technology to help dyslexic people of all ages at college, school, work or home. Providing products such as textHELP®, Dragon Naturally Speaking, Inspiration and software on learning skills such as reading, spelling, grammar, comprehension and memory. See www.iansyst.co.uk and www.dyslexic.com.

Crick Software www.cricksoft.com. Popular clicker programs can be used for sentence building, word banks, writing frames and multimedia. Lively presentations, e.g. series on Find Out and Write About includes programs on explorers, castles and animals. Also provide Clicker books and Clicker animations.

An excellent review of software for children and adults with dyslexia can be found at www.dyslexia-teacher.com/t10e.html. This international website comments on spellcheckers, electronic books, different kinds of calculators, **Wordshark** and **Clicker4** (talking word processor), **Kurzweil 3000** (which scans and reads books), **WordQ** (a writing tool that uses advanced word prediction), **textHELP®**, **Co:Writer** (which provides vocabulary, spelling, composition and revision that builds and supports skills in writing), **Write Outloud** (talking word processor – very suitable for grades 3–12), **PenFriend**, (supportive writing software featuring word prediction (predictive typing), onscreen keyboards and screen-reader speech feedback), **Dragon Naturally Speaking** (a well-reviewed dictation program which allows you to speak to your word processing program and it will type what you say – *'An invaluable program which I use every day'* (John Bradford from www.worldofdyslexia.org – another excellent resource).

As indicated earlier the role of teaching assistants is also a crucial consideration. Training is also very important in this respect. Some of the specialised training courses that they could attend include:

- Specific teaching skills needed for teaching reading, spelling and maths.
- Dealing with parents.
- Social and emotional aspects of learning, such as circle time and dealing with stress in students.
- Working with ICT.

- Study skills.
- Learning styles.
- Differentiation.
- Evaluating resources.
- Working with others.
- Understanding the reading process.
- Writing skills.

Taking the above into account the implication is that inclusion should be seen in its broadest sense, utilising the support of all types of resources as well as collaboration with parents.

The role of the community

Full inclusion can only become a reality if the whole community is included. This implies that links with community facilities such as libraries, community centres and organisations such as housing associations and co-operatives, which may not be directly involved in education, are essential, as inclusion is not only about full access to education but about social fairness and equitable distribution of resources.

School level

At the school level this requires curriculum planning and shared objectives between home and school. Consultation and planning appear to be two of the key factors that can bring about such equity and consequently full access to the curriculum.

Meeting needs

In 2001, a revised Code of Practice for England and Wales was issued by the Secretary of State for Education, giving guidance to education authorities on their duties in making special provision for pupils. This means that legally, local authorities must have regard to the provisions of the Code, therefore education authorities need to uphold the fundamental principles of the Code – entitlement to a broad curriculum, integration, pupil self-advocacy and parental involvement. The importance of the Code of Practice in England and Wales, however, is that it is enforceable by law. This means that education authorities must meet the child's educational needs and ensure that the provision identified in the statement is actually implemented.

In Scotland the approximate equivalent to a statement is the Record of Needs, although this is currently the subject of significant revision and reform. The expected legislative replacement for the record of needs is contained in the consultative document '*Additional Support for Learning*' (Scottish Executive Education Department, 2003). This document introduces a new duty on education authorities to identify and address the additional support needs of pupils and the document suggests this goes much wider than the current special educational needs framework. 'Additional support needs' in this context means *'needs for support that are additional to those which other children normally receive, in order to help a child benefit from education and so make the educational progress which is expected of him/her'*. The document suggests that education authorities will not have to assess every child formally to establish whether they have any additional support needs, but they will be expected to take steps to ensure that the reasons for a child's lack of progress are identified and appropriate action is taken. Formal assessment, therefore, is only one means that can help identify the support needs of that individual child. This has implications for children with dyslexia and clearly places more responsibility on the teacher to identify and assess their needs. Although this can be challenging for many, especially since awareness of dyslexia is still relatively low in some areas, it can help teachers adopt an approach where the key aspect is identification of the 'barriers to learning'.

In the USA the 'No Child Left Behind' legislation requires all government-run schools receiving federal funding to administer a state-wide standardised test annually to all students. The students' scores are used to determine whether the school has taught the students well. This has been not without controversy and although it can increase accountability, this can be at the expense of students at both ends of the learning continuum. This is particularly the case since there is a tendency to use the same standardized tests for all – not the ideal way to assess the progress of a student with dyslexia.

This point however has not gone unnoticed as President Barack Obama released his blueprint for reform to provide funds for states to implement a broader range of assessments to evaluate advanced academic skills, including students' abilities to conduct research, use technology, engage in scientific investigation, solve problems, and communicate effectively. This also highlights the point made earlier that inclusion is a process and it will not happen overnight.

Proactive approaches

One of the most effective ways of dealing with the issues relating to meeting the needs of all is to be proactive and minimise the challenges that often develop as the child progresses through school. For example in Scotland there is a heavy emphasis on early intervention models. This is also a feature of the US system with Response to Intervention.

Response to Intervention (RTI)

The Response to Intervention (RTI) model is an example of an evidence-based approach. The model focuses on children who are at risk of school failure and emphasises pre-referral prevention and intervention. The idea behind this is that the most appropriate type of intervention for that student can be used as early as possible to minimise the degree of potential failure.

It should be noted however that the RTI model has had its critics. Wagner (2008) argues that, 'Although identification models based on response to instruction appear potentially promising, the notion that they represent real progress for identification and intervention for children with dyslexia should be considered to be a popular myth until evidence from rigorous evaluation is available' (p. 188).

RTI can however be distinguished from traditional methods of identifying specific learning difficulties in that it allows early and intensive interventions based on learning characteristics and does not wait for children to fail before providing necessary services and supports. The major premise of RTI is that early intervening services can both prevent academic problems for many students who experience learning difficulties and determine which students actually have learning disabilities, as distinct from those whose underachievement can be attributed to other factors such as inadequate instruction.

There are a number of variations of the RTI model in practice. But generally three components can be noted: (a) the use of multiple tiers of increasingly intense interventions; (b) a problem-solving approach to identify and evaluate instructional strategies; and (c) an integrated data collection and assessment system to monitor student progress and guide decisions at every level.

The research on RTI is not conclusive. Some findings do suggest that RTI is an effective method for identifying children who are at risk of learning difficulties and for providing specialised interventions, either to ameliorate or to prevent the occurrence of learning disabilities.

Although there is some agreement about the conceptualization of RTI in terms of its key components and tiered implementation, there is often much less agreement about the nature and focus of the specialized interventions, the duration or intensity of the interventions, and the benchmarks used to determine when more intensive interventions are needed for individual children. Nevertheless the research findings suggest that RTI is a promising approach, particularly because of its focus on sound instructional principles such as effectively teaching all children, intervening early, using research-based interventions, monitoring student progress, and using assessments to inform instructional decision-making.

Dyslexia toolkit

A number of well-funded projects throughout Scotland have been implemented and these have attempted to ensure that the needs of children with dyslexia are identified early.

The Curriculum for Excellence programme in Scotland advocates that every teacher will now be a teacher of literacy. The Scottish Government has supported the funding of a Dyslexia toolkit that provides an opportunity for all teachers to further their professional development in this area. 'A key aim of the toolkit is to highlight to all class teachers that they are in the best position to identify early indicators of dyslexia and other learning difficulties. The toolkit is based on identification using the experiences and outcomes of the Curriculum for Excellence. The toolkit will offer a pathway built on the Curriculum for Excellence that all teachers will be able to follow to ensure that appropriate assessment and support are in place for learners with learning difficulties such as dyslexia when they need it' (press release May 2010). A pilot version of the toolkit has been available since January 2010 as part of the Scottish Teacher Education Committee's 'Framework for Inclusion' and can be accessed through the Framework at www.frameworkforinclusion.org.

'Say No to Failure'

Similarly in England and Wales the 'Say No to Failure' campaign has also provided considerable impetus in highlighting to government the issues surrounding dyslexia to ensure their needs are fully met within the inclusive school. For information on this ongoing campaign which is also supported by the British Dyslexia Association see www.xtraordinarypeople.com.

These legislative and government-driven initiatives should pave the way for the development of practices that can lead to an inclusive school. Much of the success of this in relation to dyslexia, however, rests on the need for effective communication between parents and school in relation to shared concerns and attitudes over the most appropriate provision and curriculum for children with dyslexia.

Issues

There are a number of important and unresolved issues relating to inclusive schooling. While there is little doubt that most agree that the concept and values associated with inclusion are of considerable merit, the actual practicalities of inclusion can be challenging. These are dealt with in the next chapter.

Additionally the inclusion debate centres on social and political issues as well as those of direct educational relevance to teachers. One of the areas of contention surrounds the most desirable provision and practices for those children identified as having special educational needs. Riddell *et al.* (2002) highlights that there has always been a desire to separate out children with special educational needs. Even those who attend mainstream school usually have special classes or have attended a dedicated onsite unit. But as Riddell points out, this has been accompanied by a desire to achieve social equity and the knowledge that children with special needs will require additional resources.

In the UK a set of materials known as the Index for Inclusion (Booth *et al.*, 2000, 2011) was developed to support the process of inclusion in schools. The Index was distributed to 26,000 primary, secondary and special schools in a government-funded initiative and was revised in 2011.

Three key areas are described in detail in the Index for Inclusion (Booth *et al.*, 2000). These relate to inclusive cultures, inclusive policies and inclusive practices. These three areas have considerable relevance for successful inclusion, but also for learning styles as each can have a role to play in helping to meet individual needs and recognising individual preferences for learning within an inclusive educational setting.

Inclusion does not happen – it is a process. Inclusion develops over time and the success of inclusion depends on the preparation and the foundations that have been put in place. Inclusion can be defined as matching the resources we have to the learning styles and educational needs of the students. This recognises the need of student-centred approaches. At the same time, while the aim of inclusion is to cater for all, it is important that the individual needs of children, particularly those children with 'additional' and special educational needs, are not overlooked. Florian (2005) suggests that 'inclusive education is not a denial of individual difference, but an accommodation of it within the structures and processes that are available to all learners' (p. 96). While children with special needs might benefit from an inclusive setting, they will require some additional considerations in terms of the structures and processes of meeting their educational, social and emotional needs.

Inclusive cultures

An inclusive culture is an important issue for children with dyslexia. They can be very sensitive to the school climate and it is important to pay a lot of attention to getting the culture and the ethos of the school right. If the culture and the climate are not inclusion-friendly, then the outcome, irrespective of policies or indeed practices, may not be successful. The Index for Inclusion (Booth *et al.*, 2000) suggests that inclusive cultures need to be created and are about building communities and establishing inclusive values. They suggest that 'it is about creating a secure, accepting, collaborating, stimulating community in which everyone is valued ... it is concerned with developing inclusive values ... [and these] guide decisions about policies and moment to moment practice so that learning of all is supported through a continuous process of school development' (p. 45).

Some of the key points include:

- The need for cultures to be created.
- The need for acceptance of all individual differences.
- The need to ensure effective communication and collaboration.
- The need for recognition that policies and practices develop over time and an acknowledgement that this development is influential in the formation of inclusive cultures.

The third edition of the *Inclusion Index* (Booth *et al.*, 2011) involves a self-review of a school's cultures, policies and practices. This self-review is an important aspect of developing effective inclusion as it ensures that the staff are taking ownership of the development and review of the inclusive process.

So what is an inclusive culture?

The index for inclusion referred to above suggests the indicators of an inclusive culture are that:

- Everyone is made welcome.
- Students help each other.
- Staff collaborate with each other.
- Staff and students treat one another with respect.
- There is a partnership between staff and parents (carers).
- All local communities are involved in the school.

These points are extremely relevant to the notion of learning styles. In fact it can be argued that by acknowledging the individual learning preferences of students, all the above points will in some way be acknowledged.

Norwich, Goodchild and Lloyd (2001) sound some caution in relation to the implementation of the Index for Inclusion. They argue that the language of the Inclusion Index might be seen to question the assumption of specialisation and special educational needs. Their concern centres on the strong focus on the social model evident in the Index. This, they suggest, raises conflicting dichotomies such as inclusive versus special needs education, and a social versus a medical model. One needs to examine how these two sets of dichotomies can be maintained within an inclusive system. Practical examples of this can be found in some special schools that have developed constructive and interactive links with mainstream schools. There is a good example of this reported by Reid (2005), who interviewed a head teacher Lannen (2002 personal interview) of a special school, the Red Rose School in England, which offers dedicated short-term provision for children with dyslexia. Most of the children admitted to the school had failed in the mainstream setting and had, not surprisingly, low levels of self-esteem, as well as low attainments. But within this specialised resource the children progress well and most of them are eventually re-admitted to mainstream schools or further education. It can be argued that within this dedicated 'special provision' the principles of inclusion are operating. All children within this environment have an entitlement to the full curriculum and to have their social, emotional and educational needs met. This is also an example of the flexible interacting continua of provision advocated by Norwich (2009).

It can be argued that there is a danger in over-supporting students with special needs in mainstream. It is important that they do not become too dependent on additional support in the mainstream as this can mean a loss of independence over the learning situation. There is an argument for suggesting that support should not be to facilitate the learning process to help students with special needs become more independent. This is particularly important for students with dyslexia as they will benefit from being able to take some control over their own learning.

Individuals with Disabilities Education Act (IDEA)

In the USA the Individuals with Disabilities Education Act (IDEA) (US Government, 2001) contains requirements that can in theory strengthen progress toward inclusive practices.

This legislation requires school districts to place students in the Least Restrictive Environment (LRE). Therefore if the IEP of a student with a disability can be implemented satisfactorily with the provision of supplementary aids and services in the regular classroom then that placement will be seen as the 'Least Restrictive Environment' for that student. Nevertheless in practice this still presents considerable challenges and tensions for teachers.

Five features of successful inclusion

1. Acknowledging differences

While it is accepted that there are common factors in dyslexia (see Reid, 2009), it is essential that these do not dictate pedagogical approaches and that the individual differences of children with dyslexia are acknowledged. It is more helpful therefore, rather than asking the question, 'What is the best approach for dyslexic children?', to ask 'What are the barriers that prevent that child from learning?' This implies that the needs of each child should be viewed within the learning situation, and environmental and curricular factors should also be considered alongside any cognitive aspects that may impinge on learning. Morton and Frith (1995) and Frith (2002) provide a framework (the causal modelling framework), that can be used to help identify these barriers. The framework consists of biological, cognitive, behavioural and environmental factors and emphasises the interactive nature of learning. The framework also emphasises the different profiles that can be associated with dyslexia. Indeed in the UK the BPS working party report on dyslexia (BPS, 1999) identified ten different hypotheses that can relate to dyslexia. Additionally the Task Force Report (Government of Ireland, 2001) indicated that 'since the difficulties presented by students with dyslexia range along a continuum from mild to severe, there is a need for a continuum of interventions and other services' (p. 31).

It is important that the identification and planning for intervention for children with dyslexia acknowledges this continuum and the individual differences associated with this as well as the role of classroom and environmental factors.

2. Recognising and acknowledging strengths

There has been considerable pressure from many groups and individuals to recognise the strengths of children with dyslexia. This is noted in the many definitions of dyslexia that are currently used (Reid, 2009). The key point is that if the barriers to literacy can be removed or minimised these strengths can be revealed. This is important as often they are overlooked or not even identified. It is important to ensure that the need to develop literacy skills, however important this may be, does not impede progress in higher-order thinking and the development of learning skills. The examples of this from West (1997, 2004; Reid, 2009) highlight the potential creativity and problem-solving skills of children and adults with dyslexia.

3. Defining inclusion

One of the key dilemmas in defining and understanding inclusion is highlighted by the need to provide common curricular objectives and a whole-class pedagogy for all yet at the same time to meet the individual and specific needs of groups of children, such as those with dyslexia. It is important, therefore, to develop inclusive models of support that can take into account the individual needs of children with dyslexia. It needs to be understood however that mainstream provision for all children, all of the time, may not be possible or desirable. This point is made by Johnson (2001) when he quotes an extract from the DfEE guidance on inclusion:

> *For most children (with special educational needs) placement in a mainstream school leads naturally on to other forms of inclusion. For those with more complex needs, the starting point should always be the question, 'Could this child benefit from education in a mainstream setting?' For some children a mainstream placement may not be right, or not right just yet.* (DfEE, 1998, p. 23).

This implies that full inclusion in a mainstream setting for some groups of children, although socially desirable, may not be educationally appropriate at a given point in time. This means that with support all children can aspire towards an inclusive educational environment, but there should not be an assumption that this is the best practice for all at every point in their school career. There are examples in practice of children with dyslexia who have initially failed in an inclusive setting, but after a period of supportive and appropriate teaching in a structured and dedicated resource for dyslexia are able to return to a mainstream setting and benefit more effectively, socially and educationally from mainstream school (Calder, 2001).

Inclusion should be seen as a comprehensive package specifically tailored for the individual to ensure social and educational benefits are maximised for all. This package is recognised in the Republic of Ireland Task Force Report when it recommends that:

special schools for students with specific learning difficulties, including dyslexia, should be developed as resource centres for special class teachers and resource teachers working with students with learning difficulties arising from dyslexia, through the development of links with local education centres. (p. 113).

Mary Warnock (2012) indicates that tension does exist between a policy that recognises the differences between different children and how the needs of each may be met, and one that seeks to regard all children as the same. This implies that inclusion does not necessarily mean that the student must be in the mainstream classroom all the time. The Centre for the Study of Inclusive Education (CSIE), which has promoted a strong position on inclusive education, stated in its inclusion charter that:

Time spent out of the ordinary classroom for appropriate individual or group work on a part-time basis is not segregation. Neither is removal for therapy or because of disruption, provided it is time-limited, for a specified purpose … Any time-out from the ordinary classroom should not affect a student's right to full membership of the mainstream (Thomas and Vaughn, 2004, p. 137).

There are also other positions that reject inclusion as necessarily being about location, placement or presence (e.g. Mary Warnock, see Chapters 2 and 7). It is important that the points indicated above are recognised in the development of school practices in inclusion.

4. Planning for practice

The learning environment is one of the most influential factors in relation to planning intervention. It is important to engage in multi-disciplinary assessment and collaboration to plan programmes which should be embedded into the whole-school curriculum. Wearmouth (2001) argues that the complexity of the issues relating to inclusion must be tackled and policymakers need to understand the long-term nature of embedding change of this nature in relation to teacher development and the provision of resources and technology. On the one hand, therefore, while inclusion can be seen as a desirable outcome in terms of equity, it can also be seen as a threat and a potential conflict between meeting the needs of individuals within a framework that has to be established to meet the needs of all.

Differentiation and curricular development are both challenges and indeed responses to meeting the needs of students with dyslexia. It is important that the learning experiences of children with dyslexia are contextualised and meaningful. Differentiation can help to make subject content appropriate and curriculum development such as developing thematic units of work can help with this. There are many examples of differentiation that have been the product of consultative collaboration within school departments (Dodds, 1996; Lucas and Guise, 2011, personal communication; Renaldi, 2011, personal communication). Ideally the needs of students with dyslexia should be met in this way and the resources and guidance on differentiation can provide a framework for the development of a differentiated approach. It is important when planning differentiated materials that the cognitive demands and learning outcomes should be made the same for all learners. Differentiation means that the routes, or modes of learning, to achieve these outcomes will be different, but not the conceptual outcomes.

5. Attainable outcomes

There is a current trend to measure educational 'progress'. This means that greater importance is placed on those variables that can be easily measured. That is not to say that such assessments cannot help to inform practice (Shiel, 2002). But it can be argued that traditional forms of assessment can disadvantage the dyslexic student because usually there is a discrepancy (possibly a significant discrepancy), between their understanding of a topic and how they are able to display that understanding in written form.

There is evidence that portfolio assessment, which has the potential to examine the performances of students with dyslexia in a much fairer way than a one-off test or national examinations, should have a greater impact on the examination system.

It can be argued that any deficit or difficulty may not lie with the student with dyslexia, but with an assessment process that is unable to accommodate to the diversity of learners. It can be advocated, therefore, that both teaching and assessment should be differentiated and diversified.

It is also important that learning outcomes should be clearly specified and attainable. For students with dyslexia this may mean some reference to additional support or examination accommodations, but the key aspect to attainable outcomes lies as much at the heart of curriculum development as it does in the assessment process.

Key issues

Some of the key factors in relation to successful inclusion and, in particular, inclusion of children with dyslexia, include:

- A commitment by the education authority and the school to an inclusive ideal.
- A realisation by staff of the widely embracing features of inclusion and the equity inherent in these features.
- Awareness of the particular specific needs associated with children with dyslexia and accommodation for these through curriculum and teaching approaches.
- Acceptance that inclusion is more than integration and that it embraces social, cultural and community equity issues as well as educational equality.
- Regard for the cultural differences in communities and families and acknowledgement that children with dyslexia require flexible approaches in assessment and teaching.
- Honouring not only the child's individual rights, but individual differences.

Comment

The five points made here – acknowledging the differences, recognising strengths, understanding inclusion, planning for practice, and attainable outcomes – highlight the challenges and the needs of children with dyslexia if full and effective inclusion is to be a reality. It is recognised that one of the most crucial elements in effective learning is self-esteem. In the wrong setting and learning environment, using inappropriate curricular and learning materials, self-esteem can be adversely affected. It is important, therefore, that while inclusion is desirable for all children, including children with dyslexia, flexibility prevails and the individual needs of children are acknowledged.

4 Curriculum access

All students with dyslexia should have full access to the curriculum. This may be very challenging in some situations, but with adaptations and considerations of the student's individual needs and strengths, it can become a reality. There are a number of factors that need to be considered in relation to curriculum access for students with dyslexia. These are:

- Obtaining relevant and accurate information to provide a full picture of the student's learning profile.
- Acknowledging the student's strengths, interests and learning preferences.
- Dealing with the challenges presented through collaborative approaches to planning learning.
- Accessing appropriate resources.

The student's learning profile

When obtaining information on the student's learning profile, it is essential that their strengths, weaknesses and learning preferences are identified. It is also necessary to identify if they have dyslexia and to do this it is preferable to have a rationale and a strategy for the assessment. Observation is a good starting point as it can give you a lead into the students' likely challenges and strengths and can point to further assessment if necessary.

The information obtained from observation and any further assessment will need to be contextualised and converted into a learning profile. From this profile the barriers to learning for that student can be noted. Importantly the next step is to highlight how these barriers can be overcome.

Overcoming Barriers to Learning – 8 factors to consider

1. The learner's specific strengths and weaknesses.

2. The learner's current level of performance in attainments.

3. Explanations for the learner's lack of progress.

4. The 'pattern of errors' noted in reading, writing and spelling.

5. The student's learning style and learning preference.

6. Areas of the curriculum that may interest and motivate the learner.

7. Specific aspects of the curriculum that are challenging for the learner.

8. The learner's level of self-esteem.

It is important to note that dyslexia and indeed the learning profile should not **only** be identified through the use of a test or tests. Assessment and the identification of dyslexia is a **process** and that 'process' involves much more than the administration of a test or group of tests. In addition to noting the students strengths, identification should also consider three aspects in particular, difficulties, discrepancies and differences, and these should relate to the classroom environment, the cultural differences, and the curriculum as well as the learning preferences of the student. The assessment therefore needs to consider the task and the curriculum as well as the learning environment and the learning experience.

Identifying needs

Assessment criteria for dyslexia: difficulties, discrepancies and differences

The central **difficulty** is usually related to the decoding (reading) or the encoding (spelling) of print, and this difficulty may be due to a range of different contributory factors. For example, some difficulties may include: phonological processing issues, visual-processing difficulties, memory factors, organizational and sequencing difficulties, motor and co-ordination difficulties, language problems or perceptual difficulties of an auditory or visual nature.

Discrepancies can become apparent when we make comparisons between decoding and reading/listening comprehension, between oral and written responses and between performances within the different subject areas of the curriculum. It is important to acknowledge the role of listening and reading comprehension in the assessment process.

It is also important to acknowledge the **differences** between individual learners. This particularly applies to children with dyslexia as they will not have identical profiles. An assessment, therefore, should also consider learning and cognitive styles as well as the learning and teaching environment. This also helps to take the child's preferences for learning into account. This in fact should be one of the aims of an assessment.

These points emphasise the view that assessment should not be carried out in isolation. It needs a context, a purpose and appropriate linkage with intervention. Similarly, teaching reading should not be carried out in isolation. Assessment therefore is the starting point but it is important that the time allocated to assessment is used appropriately and productively. That is why a range of materials should be used and that the teacher needs to be empowered to take some responsibility for the assessment process – to observe, to identify, to monitor and to plan appropriate intervention based on a solid and sound framework. A good example of this is the assessment framework developed through Dyslexia Scotland and the Scottish Government by Crombie and colleagues; see www.frameworkforinclusion.org/AssessingDyslexia (accessed October 2011).

Additionally it is necessary to take linguistic and cultural factors and differences into account. We live in a multicultural and multilingual society and this has implications for the development of tests and the administration of the assessment process.

There is no golden formula for addressing the specific learning needs of every student who experiences difficulties of a dyslexic nature because every student with dyslexia is an individual and the teaching and learning situation will also vary.

Addressing difficulties is a question of problem-solving; it is important to:

- Find out about the learner, the difficulties he/she experiences and his/her views.
- Find out about the views of the learner's family.
- Assess barriers to the student's learning in the classroom environment and in the particular curriculum area.
- Think about the requirements of the particular curriculum area.
- Reflect on what will best address those barriers to help the learner to achieve in the classroom (Reid and Green 2008).

Some of the difficulties that can present challenges in the classroom situation include both cognitive (processing of learning) and attainment (performances in the classroom) challenges. These attainment challenges are noted below.

Cognitive challenges

Working memory, short-term memory and long-term memory. Working memory is holding two or more pieces of information at the same time in short-term memory and working out a response to a problem. This would occur, for example in mental arithmetic, or when remembering lists of tasks.

The student with dyslexia can also experience difficulties with long-term memory as this requires organization and categorizing of information and this type of organizing and planning can be challenging for them.

Processing speed can also be a cognitive difficulty and very often students with dyslexia have difficulty with processing speed. They often take an indirect route to obtain a response and this may well lead to an innovative and correct response but it usually takes more time to process. They may also process visually and this can also take longer.

Automaticity involves learning an activity or a skill until it becomes automatic. That means being able to read or spell a word automatically without deliberation as often happens when a child with dyslexia decodes a word. Automaticity takes a considerable amount of time to acquire and will need substantial 'overlearning'. This is one of the essential prerequisites for learners with dyslexia – overlearning.

Metacognitive awareness involves being aware of how one is learning and the most effective way of learning new material. Essentially this involves learning to learn and can be challenging for students with dyslexia. They may choose inefficient strategies to tackle a problem and may not be able to transfer existing learning to new situations. This could apply to spelling when learning spelling rules and word groups. Metacognition also involves the ability to self-monitor and self-correct. This is an important skill to teach children with dyslexia as they may not be able to do this automatically.

Attainments

It is also important to consider the pattern of attainments. Looking at this in detail can provide clues on the barriers the student is experiencing and how to deal with these in the classroom. Some of these are shown below.

- Listening comprehension, especially when working under timed conditions.
- Maths, especially when undertaking complex working-out of problems.
- Phonological memory.
- Reading comprehension – both silent and oral reading.
- Reading fluency.
- Lack of automaticity in reading.
- Decoding.

These challenges provide a starting point on how these needs can be addressed. Some priorities for intervention can be worked out. An example is shown below.

Priorities for intervention

- Decoding skills.
- Developing sight words.
- Self-monitoring of comprehension.
- Expressive writing skills, including grammar and sentence conventions.
- Spelling.
- Developing inferential language skills.
- Developing word-processing skills.

Formative assessment

An interesting finding from the research is that 'there is **no** evidence that increasing the amount of testing will enhance learning' (Assessment Reform Group, 1999, p. 2). This might explain why in many countries there has been a shift in emphasis from assessment methods that serve only summative purposes to more formative types of assessment. Results from externally imposed summative tests, especially where there are very high stakes attached to the results, can have very negative effects on students. Teachers often feel they have to devote considerable time to practise test-taking rather than to using assessment to support learning. Where this is the case, students, especially those with dyslexia, can become over-anxious and demoralised. This means they will view assessment as something to fear – as something that can stigmatise them as failures within their peer group.

Formative assessment can provide learners with dyslexia with the right kind of feedback and can take much of the stress out of assessment. Assessment should be a 'learning' experience not a 'testing' one!

Improving learning through assessment can depend on five factors:

- Effective feedback.
- Active involvement of students in their own learning.

- Adjusting teaching to take account of the results of assessment.
- Recognition of the influence assessment has on motivation and self-esteem.
- The need for students to be able to self-assess and understand how to develop their own learning.

Development of formative assessment

Ongoing formative assessment can therefore provide teachers with a range of opportunities to obtain important information on the learner. Some points are noted below.

Noticing

- Notice what is happening during learning activities. It is important to observe interactions as well as results.
- Recognise the direction of the student's learning – is the student heading in the right direction and does he or she comprehend the task?
- Are they likely to obtain the correct response? Are there opportunities for extending their learning?

Reflective practitioners

The above would be considered an important aspect of being a reflective practitioner. 'Noticing' and 'adjusting' are terms that are used in association with the term 'reflective practitioner' and this is what is needed to support students with dyslexia.

Reflective practitioners notice what is different or unusual about patterns of progress in student learning. They also provide feedback to students and this can be very effective particularly when it:

- Focuses on the tasks and the actual learning process and not on any student deficit.
- Informs students that they are on the right track or can put them on the right track.
- Includes suggestions that help the student to scaffold* their learning and know the type of supports to access.
- Is provided frequently and there is an opportunity for the student to act on the feedback provided.

Feedback that connects directly to specific goals related to the task the student is working on can help him or her focus more productively on new goals and next learning steps.

Assessment and intervention

It is important to ensure that the assessment process and results from any tests used are contextualised in relation to the curriculum and the nature of the child's learning situation. Sometimes factors within the classroom and the materials that are being used may account for the difficulties the child is displaying as much as the child's own attributes.

---

*   Scaffolding is a term that is widely used in education to describe a learning process that can promote deeper learning and develop connections between previous and new learning.

Came and Reid (2008) tackle the issue of assessing literacy from the view of identifying concern and empowering the teacher to be in a position to do this. In their publication *Concern, Assess, Provide (CAP) It All* (Came and Reid 2008), the authors provide a range of materials that can be used in the classroom context and focus directly on the student's current work.

They ask the key question 'What is literacy?' and suggest that the answer to that question will determine the selection of information to undertake an assessment. This can mean addressing the functional aspects of literacy (technical) or the purpose of literacy (meaning). One of the important aspects of this is to have efficient and effective monitoring mechanisms in place to ensure that all aspects of the reading process are addressed. Unlike some other tests, they include assessment of children's inferential understanding of text as well as the literal meaning of the passage. Identifying the inferences in texts is an important element for developing higher-order thinking and processing skills and is particularly important for children with dyslexia as often their main focus tends to be on mastering the bottom-up sub-skills of reading and the inferential meanings of the text are sometimes lost. This can also lead to developing self-assessment and metacognitive skills such as those indicated earlier in this chapter. The process envisaged by Came and Reid is shown below in Table 4.1.

Table 4.1 Assessing reading ability and skills (from Came and Reid 2008)

1. **Background information**: a summary of the pupil's reading-related information based on scores of standardised achievement tests, criterion referenced tests, and basal end-of-book tests. The current reading status of the pupil is indicated, as is any supplementary help he/she is receiving.
2. **Purpose of referral**: a synopsis of the reasons for the request for diagnostic evaluation. Included are comments of specific reading concerns expressed by classroom teachers, resource personnel, school psychologists, parents, etc.
3. **Testing**: a brief description of the pupil's behaviour and displayed attitude during the testing battery, and the specific areas of reading that were tested.
4. **Diagnostic summary**: an explanation of the results of tests administered in each reading skill area:
    A. *Emergent/readiness skills*: *Checks for*: beginning reading skills. *Deficiency suggests*: difficulty understanding and following directions.
    B. *Auditory skills*: *Checks for*: hearing and remembering sounds in words. *Deficiency suggests*: difficulty understanding and following oral directions, instructions, class discussions, and establishing sound/symbol relationships necessary for phonic instruction.
    C. *Visual skills*: *Checks for*: seeing and remembering printed or written material. *Deficiency suggests*: difficulty remembering letters in words – consequently writing words with letters reversed or jumbled or perceiving words incorrectly for decoding.
    D. *Word recognition skills*: *Checks for*: recognising and applying the sounds for the symbols, such as phonic generalizations and syllabic principles. *Deficiency suggests*: difficulty reading fluently, with many mispronunciations.
    E. *Language and vocabulary development*: *Checks for*: understanding and expressing adequate language and the concepts of written words. *Deficiency suggests*: difficulty understanding written material and classroom instructions.

> *F. Oral reading/comprehension*: *Checks for*: decoding ability, fluency, accuracy, and comprehension. **Silent Reading/Comprehension:** *Checks for*: understanding of vocabulary and comprehension. **Listening Comprehension:** *Checks for*: processing information presented orally and comparing listening to oral/silent reading ability
>
> 5. **Interpretation of diagnosis**: the tester's opinion of what might be blocking the pupil's reading growth – the reading weaknesses and strengths the teacher must take into consideration in adjusting the curriculum to meet the pupil's needs.
> 6. **Learning goals:** a concise list of goals the tester has devised to improve the pupil's learning to read.
> 7. **Teaching recommendations:** specific suggestions and methods to aid in providing appropriate instruction in order for the pupil to attain the goals.
> 8. **Learning activities**: suggestions designed to help you understand and assist the pupil in coping.

Reproduced with permission of *Learning Works*, Came and Reid (2008).

It is important to observe the student's preferred mode of learning. Many learners with dyslexia will show preferences and skills in a number of modalities. This means that multi-sensory teaching is crucial as it will accommodate all the different modalities of learning.

Table 4.2 Barriers to Learning

Cognitive	Educational
• differences in methods of information processing • phonological processing • limited working memory capacity • sequencing and spatial awareness • processing speed • automaticity • metacognitive awareness.	• lack of scaffolding to develop new learning • lack of opportunities for overlearning • reading levels of tasks • copying work out from the board or book • pace of learning • too much text on page • restricted vocabulary • confusing similar-sounding words.
Emotional	**Environmental**
• lack of confidence and low self-esteem • anxiety and stress • learned helplessness • on-task behaviour • social communication • time pressure.	• lack of visual aids/visual prompts • limited access to technology • lighting • background noise • ambience – formal/informal • lack of opportunities for group work.

Note in Table 4.2 that the barriers and potential barriers that are shown can potentially prevent the learner from full curriculum access. But all can be dealt with through pre-planning and forethought as well as some knowledge and understanding of what dyslexia actually is and how it impacts on the individual student.

Table 4.3 identifies some ways to deal with these barriers.

Table 4.3 Dealing with the barriers to learning

Cognitive	Educational
Acknowledge that not all students will be able to process through listening (auditory mode) – students with dyslexia will benefit from kinaesthetic activities (experience). **Phonological processing** – it is widely agreed that this is the key component of teaching reading to dyslexic learners. Need to ensure that a multisensory reading programme is available. **Limited working memory capacity** – it is important to provide instructions or tasks one at a time. If too many things are to be remembered it will overcrowd working memory and the information will be lost. **Sequencing and spatial awareness** – it is important to be aware of this as this can have implications for following instructions and following lists. It can also have implications for sport and games. **Processing speed** – this can be a real challenge for learners with dyslexia, on account of their processing style. Activities that are timed, if structured, can help with processing speed, as can some computer games. Copying information from the board or from a book can also be challenging and should preferably be avoided or additional time allowed for it. **Automaticity** – the key strategy to help with automaticity is overlearning. Although this can sound quite simplistic, it is important for students with dyslexia. They need a great deal of repetition and practice before a skill can become automatic. **Metacognitive awareness** – this involves thinking about thinking and being aware of the best way to learn for the individual. It is important to talk through the learning process with the individual student – even getting them to think aloud as they tackle the task.	**Lack of scaffolding to develop new learning** – scaffolding is crucial. It is a process by which a teacher provides students with a temporary framework for learning. A suitably structured scaffold will facilitate the student's independent learning. A popular way of doing this is to model an activity for the learner, providing advice and examples and guiding the student's learning until he/she can perform the task independently. **Lack of opportunities for overlearning** – as indicated in the cognitive component, overlearning is important for automaticity. It is crucial to seek out all opportunities to ensure overlearning takes place and to allow time for that. **Reading levels of tasks** – it is important to ensure that the reading level is right for the student. It is a good idea to use books that have a lower reading level as this will help to develop reading fluency. The books by Barrington Stoke are excellent for this (see www.barringtonstoke.co.uk). **Copying work out from board or book** – avoid this. Instead provide printed information. **Too much text on page** – presentation is very important. When providing a worksheet ensure that you use visuals and leave space – do not overcrowd the page. **Restricted vocabulary** – although students may have a sound oral vocabulary and a good understanding of words, this is usually not the case in written work. They may actually show a restricted vocabulary and will benefit from being provided with key words. **Confusing similar-sounding words** – this can be a problem for secondary students as often there is a new 'technical' vocabulary to be learnt and some of the words may sound the same.

Table 4.3 continued

Emotional	Environmental
Lack of confidence and low self-esteem – it is important to provide opportunities for success. Self-esteem will be enhanced with success and this can make the student more confident. All opportunities for success need to be considered.	**Lack of visual aids/visual prompts** – it is important that the learning environment is dyslexia friendly. Usually a visually stimulating classroom is preferred, although there should be opportunities for quiet and low-stimulation areas.
Anxiety and stress – informal learning situations can help to reduce anxieties. Give the student some choice and flexibility. This can help learning be more informal and less stressful. The buddy system may also help with this.	**Limited access to technology** – technology can be a great benefit for children with dyslexia. It is important to ensure that they have access to computer games and activities that can help with keyboarding skills.
Learned helplessness – the best way to deal with this is to prevent it from occurring in the first place. Once the student starts to fail it is difficult to reverse and the feelings of failure the student experiences will take some time to overcome. This is why early intervention is so important.	**Lighting and background noise** – it is important to get the environment right for the learner. Usually students with dyslexia will prefer low lighting and often music in the background. It is important to get the most effective music for different activities. (see www.mozarteffect.com).
On-task behaviour – a great deal can be learnt about students by observing their on-task behaviours – the strategies they use, the length of their attention span and the type of situations they attend to best. This could be when they are active and interactive rather than when they are listening.	**Structure – formal/informal** – ideally the layout of the classroom allows for a blend of formal and informal settings. Many dyslexic learners need a structure and quite a formal setting, but at the same time it is important not to restrict them too much. So it is important to have a creative area that is less formal and involves more choice and flexibility.
Social communication – often students with dyslexia can obtain success from their peer group and become quite skilled socially. It is important to provide a key role for them in group work.	**Lack of opportunities for group work** – students with dyslexia need to have opportunities for group work. Often they learn best in this way, but it is important that some consideration is given the composition of the group. They need people in the group who can reflect and encourage as this can be stimulating for them. It is a good idea to experiment a little with the group composition.
Time pressure – if at all possible this should be avoided altogether. Students with dyslexia will not react well to time pressures and usually will require additional time to complete many tasks.	

In many ways identifying and dealing with barriers to learning involves a problem-solving approach. Once the problem has been identified then solutions can be sought. The important point about this is that it is possible to devise a framework that can be followed by other teachers in the school. It helps to clarify the actual problem and importantly how to monitor it in the classroom situation. An example is shown below.

A problem-to-solution approach

1. Clarify the concern
   - Define the problem.
   - Who has the problem?
   - Why are there concerns?
   - What do we want to achieve?
   - What strategies have been attempted which work/don't work?
2. Obtain the evidence
   - Look at the full range of evidence already available.
   - Reassess the difficulty (problem).
   - Establish a starting point for intervention or further assessment.
3. Planning for learning
   - What strategies/programmes will be used?
   - Who will implement them?
   - What are the specific short-term targets?
   - What is the role of parents.
   - Who will monitor progress?
   - How will progress be measured?
4. Action/Implementation
   - What is going well?
   - When is it working?
   - Has progress been measured?
   - Is progress evident?
   - Has monitoring informed future targets?
   - Should the plan continue?
   - What are the future targets?
5. Monitor/review
   - Have formal reviews been established?
   - What is the frequency of reviews?
   - Has self-monitoring and self-assessment been considered?

Source: Adapted from Came and Reid (2008).

The purpose of the above is to be precise about the challenges the student is experiencing without the need to resort to a label. A label may well be available but it is not essential using this formula.

Effective learning

Much of good practice for students with dyslexia essentially focuses on effective learning. Effective learning involves a number of interactive cognitive and learning activities. The learner can control these activities to make learning efficient and effective. This however can be difficult for students with dyslexia as often they become too dependent on a teacher, or support teacher. It is crucial therefore that the skills required for effective learning are acquired at an early age.

There are some common strands for effective learning that can be considered by teachers. These include:

- **Understanding**: the learner needs be able to understand the requirements of the task.
- **Planning**: the learner needs to be able to identify the key points and be able to work out a learning plan.
- **Action**: the learner needs to have the resources and skills to carry out the task.
- **Transfer of learning**: previous learning should help to provide a plan and strategies for tackling new tasks.

Some important factors to consider include:

1. The need to anticipate the barriers to learning the student with dyslexia may encounter.
2. The need to accumulate knowledge of the learner's individual learning preferences.
3. The need to differentiate the task through presentation and through outcome.
4. The important consideration of assisting students with dyslexia to take responsibility for their own learning and to be able to monitor their own progress.

These points above are important for learners with dyslexia because it is possible to prevent failure if these points are adhered to. For example it is possible to anticipate the barriers to learning for students with dyslexia. For example in relation to memory students with dyslexia can have difficulty with the following:

- Remembering instructions.
- Remembering sequences.
- Remembering equipment.
- Confusing time, dates and days of the week.
- Remembering rules and patterns.

It is therefore possible to prevent memory from being a problem by ensuring that when setting tasks any undue burden on memory is minimised.

The same considerations apply to processing speed. The following can be challenging for students with dyslexia, so this should be taken into account when planning learning and developing materials.

Students with dyslexia have difficulty in the following:

- Handling time pressures.
- Working at a fast pace.
- Using efficient methods of learning.
- Completing work without the need to check and re-check.
- Keeping on track and keeping the purpose of a task in mind.

It should be possible to take these factors into account and therefore minimise the possibility of the learner with dyslexia failing in the inclusive context.

Some learning strategies that can facilitate curriculum access are shown on the next page.

Curriculum access: learning strategies

1. **Metacognition**: this essentially means thinking about thinking and has an important role in how children learn. This can be vital to help dyslexic children clarify concepts, ideas and situations and therefore make learning and reading more meaningful. This also helps in the transfer of learning from one situation to another. Flavell (1979) greatly influenced the field of metacognition and its applications to the classroom, and since then metacognition has been given considerable prominence in schools and in assessment and curriculum activities.

   There have been a number of models implemented in relation to metacognition.

   One that is well-established and relevant to the learning of dyslexic children is that proposed by Brown *et al.* (1986). This model contains four main variables relevant to learning:

   - Text – the material to be learnt.
   - Task – the purpose of reading.
   - Strategies – how the learner understands and remembers information.
   - Characteristics of the learner – prior experience, background knowledge, interests and motivation.

2. **The encouragement of control over learning**: This is important as it can facilitate self-confidence and enhance learning skills. This can be practised with reading, spelling and creative writing.

3. **Comprehension-monitoring behaviour**: Wray (1994) defines differences between good and poor readers. He suggests that the main difference relates to comprehension-monitoring behaviour. For example, good readers generate questions while they read, are able to transfer what they read into mental images, reread if necessary and actively comprehend while they read. Poor readers, on the other hand, lack a clear purpose of reading, view reading as essentially a decoding task and seldom reread or actively comprehend while they read.

4. The use of **discussion** to activate prior knowledge needs to be considered. This can also enhance metacognitive skills. The teacher may have to make prior knowledge explicit or the opportunity may be lost to the student.

5. **Visual imagery**: strategies such as visual imagery, obtaining the main ideas from text, developing concepts through Mind Mapping© and self-questioning, all of which attempt to relate previous knowledge with the new material to be learned. It is important that dyslexic students are encouraged to use these strategies, otherwise they may become too entrenched in the actual process of reading rather than in the meaning and purpose of the activity.

6. **Meaningful experiences and thinking aloud**: cue cards that contain ideas for thinking aloud can stimulate self-questioning during a creative writing exercise. Thinking aloud can also help the student keep track of the learning process and monitor the progress being made.

7. **Reciprocal teaching**: Reciprocal teaching refers to a procedure that both monitors and enhances comprehension by focusing on processes relating to questioning, clarifying, summarising and predicting (Palincsar and Brown, 1984). This is an interactive process. Brown (1993) describes the procedure for reciprocal teaching as one that is initially led by the teacher. The teacher leads the discussion by asking questions, and this generates additional questions from participants. The questions

are then clarified by teacher and participants together. The discussion is then summarised by the teacher or participants, following which a new 'teacher' is selected by the participants to lead the discussion on the next section of the text.

8. **Think to read**: Oczkus (2004) cites MacLaughlin and Allen's (2002) example of the broad framework of eight strategies that they feel is essential for teaching students to understand what they are reading:

    1. Pre-viewing – activating prior knowledge, predicting and setting a purpose.
    2. Self-questioning – generating questions to guide reading.
    3. Making connections – relating reading to self, text and world.
    4. Visualising – creating mental pictures.
    5. Knowing how words work – understanding words through strategic vocabulary development, including the use of graphophonic, syntactic and semantic cueing systems.
    6. Monitoring – asking whether text makes sense and clarifying by adapting strategic processes.
    7. Summarizing – synthesizing important ideas.
    8. Evaluating – making judgements.

    Source: Quoted at www.think2read.co.uk/reciprocal-reading-framework.htm.

9. **Scaffolding** – Scaffolding refers to supports that are developed to enhance understanding of learning. This may be in the form of the teacher either providing the information or generating appropriate responses through questioning and clarifying. The supports are then withdrawn gradually when the learner has achieved the necessary understanding to continue with less support. Cudd and Roberts (1994) observed that poor readers were not automatically making the transfer from book language to their own writing. As a result the students' writing lacked the precise vocabulary and varied syntax that was evident during reading. To overcome this difficulty Cudd and Roberts introduced a scaffolding technique to develop both sentence sense and vocabulary. They focused on sentence expansion by using vocabulary from the children's readers; using these as sentence stems encouraged sentence expansion. The procedure used involved:

    - Selection of vocabulary from basal reader.
    - Embedding this vocabulary into sentence stems.
    - Selecting particular syntactic structures to introduce the stems.
    - Embedding the targeted vocabulary into sentence stems to produce complex sentences.
    - Discussing the sentence stems, including the concepts involved.
    - Completing a sentence using the stems.
    - Repeating the completed sentence, providing oral reinforcement of both the vocabulary and the sentence structure.
    - Encouraging illustration of some of their sentences, helping to give the sentence a specific meaning.

10. **Transfer of Skills** – Transfer of skills can best be achieved when emphasis is firmly placed on the process of learning and not the product. This encourages children to reflect on learning and encourages the learner to interact with other learners and with the teacher. In this way effective study skills can help to activate learning and

provide the student with a structured framework for effective learning. Nisbet and Shucksmith (1986) describe one example of such a framework that focuses on preparation, planning and reflection. Preparation looks at the goals of the current work and how these goals relate to previous work. Planning looks at the skills and information necessary in order to achieve these goals. The reflection phase assesses the quality of the final piece of work, asking such questions as: 'What did the children learn from the exercise and to what extent could the skills gained be transferred to other areas?'

11. **Encourage use of self-assessment** – when tackling a new task does the child demonstrate self-assessment by asking questions such as:

- Have I done this before?
- How did I tackle it?
- What did I find easy?
- What was difficult?
- Why did I find it easy or difficult?
- What did I learn?
- What do I have to do to accomplish this task?
- How should I tackle it?
- Should I tackle it the same way as before?

12. **Retelling** – Ulmer and Timothy (2001) developed an alternative assessment framework based on retelling as an instructional and assessment tool. This indicated that informative assessment of a child's comprehension could take place by using criteria relating to how the child retells a story.
    Ulmer and Timothy suggested the following criteria:

- Textual (what the child remembered).
- Cognitive (how the child processed the information).
- Affective (how the child felt about the text).

Their two-year study indicated that whilst all the teachers in the study had made assessments for textual information, only 31 per cent had looked for cognitive and 25 per cent for affective indicators. They also found that those teachers who did go beyond the textual level found rich information. So for example use of the retelling method of assessment could provide evidence of a child's 'creative side'. Teachers discovered that children could go 'beyond expectations when given the opportunity'. This is a good example of how looking for alternative means of assessing can better reveal the child's understandings of text and promote development thinking. On the other hand, where assessment instruments are restricted (examining what the child may be expected to know, often only at a textual level), this could exclude other rich sources of information that could be very telling about the child's thinking, both cognitive and affective, and could bolster teaching practice.

13. **Active learning** – this can help the learner retain and understand new information to be learnt. The more active the learner is, the more likely the information is understood and retained. This activity could be in the form of discussion but it could also be in drama form and first-person speech. This can be more easily achieved in some subjects such as history where first person and drama can be used to re-enact historical events.

14. **Discussion** – for many learners with dyslexia discussion is the most effective means of retaining and understanding information. Discussion can make the information meaningful and can help the learner experiment with ideas and views. It is this experimentation that helps learners extend their thinking and learning.

15. **Mnemonics** – this can be auditory or visual, or both auditory and visual. Auditory mnemonics may take the form of rhyming or alliteration, while visual mnemonics can be used by relating the material to be remembered to a familiar scene, such as the classroom.

16. **Mind Mapping**© – this was developed by Buzan (1993) to help children and adults develop their learning skills and utilize as much of their abilities as possible. The procedure is now widely used and can extend one's memory capacity and develop lateral thinking (Buzan, 1993). It can be a simple or a sophisticated strategy depending on how it is developed and used by the individual. It is used to help the learner to remember a considerable amount of information and encourages students to think of, and develop, the main ideas of a passage or material to be learned. It adopts in many ways some of the principles already discussed in relation to schemata theory.

Tips for the teacher

Summary of support strategies for children with dyslexia
(Adapted from Thomson, Moira (2008), *Supporting Students with Dyslexia in Secondary Schools,* Abingdon, Routledge, p. 137).

Reading for information
- Use a range of modes of presenting information – not just print.
- Highlight in **bold** the key information.
- Small group discussion is particularly valuable for the learner with dyslexia.
- Use video, audio or ICT presentation.
- Give specific line, page and paragraph references. Do not assume they can use contents and index pages.
- Allow coloured overlay use if students prefers that.
- Enlarge print and use increased line spacing so the page looks more appealing.

Reading aloud
- **Never** ask the student to read aloud.
- **Key information** should be read aloud only by a teacher or competent reader.

Writing tasks
- Never use blank notebooks/paper except for drawing.
- Provide copies of diagrams and charts.
- Provide a framework for extended writing – e.g. writing frames, www.warwick.ac.uk/staff/D.J.Wray/Ideas/frames.html.
- Allow alternatives to handwriting:
  - scribe
  - laptop computer
  - word processor
  - dictaphone
  - voice recorder.

Copying

- Provide printed notes in advance.
- Make photocopies of notes.
- Scan text into a computer.
- Identify a copying partner.
- Encourage all pupils to work together.
- Ensure that copies of learning materials are made as soon as possible after a lesson.

Organisation

- Do not give complex verbal instructions.
- Give only one instruction at a time.
- Structure set tasks.
- Be realistic in setting tasks.
- Encourage correct use of homework diary and involve parents.
- Do not automatically set unfinished reading or writing as homework.

Effects of fatigue

- Give short, well-defined tasks.
- Keep task structure simple.
- Set time-limits for tasks.
- Teach appropriate pacing.
- Vary the types of tasks.
- Change activities often to create time for 'rests'.
- Set clearly defined targets.
- Create an opportunity for purposeful movement.

Different learning styles

- Present information in a variety of modes – video, ICT, teacher talk, etc.
- Present information in a variety of formats – text, tables, diagrams.
- Allow opportunities for active learning by – discussion, role play, research / investigation, etc.

Number

- Issue square/lined paper.
- Allow the use of calculators for all number work.
- Provide training in the use of calculators.
- Issue templates of shapes to emphasise their different properties.
- Make addition and multiplication grids readily available.
- Use a variety of approaches (including computer games) to develop and reinforce number facts.

Curriculum access: the learning context

When identifying and assessing the nature and degree of the difficulty experienced by the child, it is important to take into account the learning context.

This context, depending on the learner's preferred style, can either exacerbate the difficulty or minimise the problem. The contextual factors below should, therefore, be considered:

- Classroom environment.
- Teaching style.
- The nature of the task.
- Materials/resources.

Wearmouth and Reid (2002) suggest that in order to plan appropriate teaching approaches for children with dyslexia and other special needs there has been a move away from the solely 'medical' model of difficulties in learning to one that recognizes their interactive nature. This envisages a broader concept of the nature of 'special needs' and how these can be identified and addressed.

This is essentially an 'interactive model', and the focus is on the barriers to pupils' learning that may arise as a result of the interaction between the characteristics of the student and what is offered through teaching and the available resources. So while cognitive assessment of pupils who may have dyslexia is important, it is also crucial to include interactive aspects in the assessment criteria. Therefore, it is important to assess the learning environment in which pupils acquire literacy. Difficulties in literacy development can be seen as a function of the interaction between within-child and environmental factors. It therefore follows that there must be an assessment of both the student's characteristics and also of the learning environment.

Environmental factors can be examined by observing how the child performs in different settings with different types of support. This will provide useful information when developing programmes for the student to help them use their own learning style. The proforma example below suggests that planning for learning and preparing differentiated materials needs to incorporate information from a range of sources. It is also important to set this against the learning context. Therefore while completing this type of proforma it is also important to consider the environment and how adjustments might need to be made.

Reid (2007) provides a continuum of learning environments from very structured to very informal. He suggests we need to consider the following factors:

- Layout – the organisation of classroom furniture.
- Design of chairs and desks.
- Position of teacher's desk in relation to the students.
- Arrangement of the students' desks.
- Flexibility in being able to move and adjust the layout of the classroom.
- Location of the classroom in relation to other classrooms in the school.
- Colour and shape of the room.
- Amount of light.
- Amount of available space.

Dockrell and McShane (1993) suggest that the environment and the learners' interaction with the environment can play a crucial role. They suggest that an analysis of the interaction between the learner and the environment can provide a helpful guide for the teacher and this type of analysis can have particular implications for students with dyslexia. Often for children with learning difficulties such as dyslexia, the environment

PLANNING FOR DIFFERENTIATED LEARNING

1. Learning Outcomes (from the IRPs)*	Assessment for data collection (teacher records) - Performance Standards, checklists, journals, observations, portfolios etc.

2. Content (concepts, vocabulary, facts)	Skills

3. Activate -Focus Activity (to activate and engage the learner)	Assessment for Learning (to inform instruction)	☐ Brainstorm ☐ Journals ☐ Quiz, test ☐ K,W,L** ☐ Draw It ☐ Survey ☐ _____ ☐ _____

4. Acquire *Whole group and/or small group *Instruction is differentiated to ensure each student meets expectations	☐ Inquiry ☐ Project ☐ Presentation ☐ Demonstration ☐ Jigsaw ☐ Video ☐ Field Trip ☐ Guest Speaker ☐ Text ☐ Technology Support

5. Apply and Adjust *Grouping decisions (random, task, heterogeneous, homogeneous, interest, etc.) Who will help?　　　Who will help? How will they support?　How will they support?	☐ Learning Centres ☐ Projects ☐ Contracts ☐ Compact/Enrichment ☐ Problem Based ☐ Inquiry ☐ Research ☐ Independent Study ☐ _____ ☐ _____

6. Assess and Monitor *Criteria for meeting expectations	☐ Presentation ☐ Demonstration ☐ Products ☐ Log, journal ☐ Checklist ☐ Portfolio ☐ Rubric ☐ Quiz, test ☐ _____

Figure 4.1

Source: Reproduced with permission from Nanson, J. (2011), Learning Support Services Handbook, SD41, Burnaby, BC.

---

*　IRP (The Integrated Resource Package) combines four key elements of learning to form a functional curriculum overview document and is a component of educational policy in the province of British Columbia, Canada.

**　KWL is an acronym used to describe a writing programme based on the following; What I Know, What I Want to Know and What I have Learned.

can have an important role to play. If it is too structured they may feel inhibited and not able to take any risks with learning. If it is too loose and liberal they may not be able to work effectively because of lack of structure. It is worthwhile discussing this with students and making sure learners obtain some data on their own learning styles.

There are many manifestations of learning style and the learning environment. One method however that can be used to begin the observation process is to select one of the learning aspects and progress from there. Insights usually become greater as observation progresses. Information on learning styles can also be obtained by asking the student questions about their own preferences for learning. This can be achieved with very young children as well as secondary-aged students. Students are usually aware of their own preferences, for example if they prefer to learn with background music or if they prefer silence when studying.

While it is important to recognize individual differences among students, it is also important to consider that some general strategies can apply to all, including students with dyslexia. These whole-class approaches are very useful in supporting the student access the full curriculum. These will be discussed in detail in the following chapter.

5 Strategies and practical approaches

This chapter discusses a range of strategies that can be used in a whole-class situation. This is often the reality in an inclusive school. Specialized small-group or one-on-one approaches are necessary for some children, but these need to be supplemented with strategies that can be used independently by the student. Often these strategies benefit all children and not only those with specific needs.

Reading for information

Use a range of information sources

It is important to ensure that print is not the only source of important information – use tapes, discussion, movies and talks – all can provide information and are very likely more accessible than print for the learner with dyslexia.

Highlight key information

Students with dyslexia often prefer to learn through the use of colour – it is a good idea to highlight key information in colour. It is important however that you should not ask students to read aloud – unless they volunteer.

Discussion

Students with dyslexia often need to discuss what they have read in order to fully understand it. This verbalisation process is important for them. Encourage small-group discussion as a means of developing understanding and reporting on what they have read.

Overlearning

It is important to appreciate that students with dyslexia will need overlearning. Reading can therefore be reinforced through the use of videos, movies and pictures. This can help to embed some of the important points. It can also help with retention and recall.

Presentation

Reading for information will be easier if the material is well presented. You need to ensure that materials are legible. This can be done by using coloured paper rather than white and larger print size with double-line or line-and-a-half spacing. The student may also want to use coloured overlays.

Reading comprehension

For many students with dyslexia, reading comprehension can present some challenges. They would have good oral comprehension if the material were to be discussed with them, but when reading they often get lost in the decoding tasks and comprehension plays a secondary role. It is important to provide them with prompts to encourage and promote comprehension.

Some questions that can help with comprehension after reading are shown below.

- What did you enjoy about the book?
- Was there anything you found confusing about the book?
- Was the plot easy to follow – why/why not?
- What do you think the author was trying to tell the reader?
- Did you like the way the author described the setting?
- What could have been done to create a better picture for you?
- Was this believable? Has the information in the text been distorted or oversimplified?

Self-questioning skills for comprehension

Ideally we should be encouraging students to take responsibility for their own learning. This involves students directing their own learning initially through self-questioning.

Some self-questions may include.

- What have I got to do here?
- Do I understand the task?
- What is my plan for completing this reading/task?
- What do I already know about this topic?
- How am I doing?
- Do I need any more information?
- Can I summarise, in my own words, what I have read?

These questions will aid comprehension of the task and allow learners to take more control over their own learning. This is particularly important for students with dyslexia as it is too easy for them to allow the support teacher or the class teacher to direct their learning for them.

Pre-reading discussion

It is important to engage in pre-reading discussion with children before they start reading the text. There is a body of research that suggests that pre-reading discussion is one of the best predictors of a successful outcome in a reading activity.

Some questions that can provide a framework for pre-reading discussion are shown below.

Pointers for pre-reading discussion

- Where does the story take place?
- Time period?
- Main characters/anything unusual about the main characters?
- How does the story start?
- What should the learner look out for in the story?
- How does the book/story relate to the learner's previous knowledge/experience?

It might be more effective if the parent reads the passage first to the child, or perhaps uses paired reading.

It is also a good idea to monitor comprehension and to ensure the reader has understood the key points of the book or story. This could be carried out at regular intervals and for some children it will be necessary to do this at short intervals, such as after every paragraph, page or part of a chapter, depending on the child's level of reading. It is important that parents are aware of this; otherwise the child may spend quite a bit of time and effort reading but get very little from the book.

It is important that parents realize the importance of monitoring comprehension. This can come naturally and effortlessly for many readers. There are many strategies they may use to monitor their comprehension without recognizing that is what they are doing. They may slow down when reading text that they don't understand, they may reread, look up a word in the dictionary, look for context clues, relate the text to their own experience or background knowledge and all because they realise they have stopped comprehending and need to do something to get back on track. Many students are so busy decoding and reading for accuracy that they don't actually realise they are not comprehending. They don't have the insights to monitor their own comprehension. Parents can help by reading with their child and stopping regularly to check and make sure the child still comprehends. Then they can encourage the child to use the same strategies when they are reading alone so that eventually the child learns to monitor their comprehension independently. 'Reciprocal Teaching', a reading strategy created by Palincsar and Brown (1984) is a powerful tool in helping children with comprehension monitoring. It looks at a structured approach to reading with your child while enabling the child to monitor their comprehension through a four-step process: summarizing, questioning, clarifying and predicting.

This approach is often used by teachers in the classroom but can also be used successfully when reading one-on-one with a parent. To begin the process of reciprocal teaching, the parent reads a few paragraphs from the reading, then summarizes for the child what he/she has read, The parent then clarifies any concepts that may be confusing or words that may not be understood, asks a few questions about the passage and then makes a prediction about what will happen next. The child then takes a turn reading and goes through the same four steps of summarizing, clarifying, questioning and predicting. The exact order of the steps is not important but it may be useful to make up cue cards with visuals for each of the four steps. It is also important to recognize the different levels of comprehension and be sure to ask questions that go beyond the literal meaning. Many children can answer literal questions which reflect specific pieces of information written in the text but struggle with levels that go beyond a literal level. Questions which are creative may ask the child to change the ending to a story, or ask what they would have done if they were in the same situation as one of the characters. They require the child to use their creativity to think of an answer. A critical question will ask the child to make judgements about the author, the characters or the way the story is written. One of the most difficult types of questions will be at an inferential level. These questions require the child to infer meaning from information in the story that is not directly stated. This is a very important level of comprehension that should not be overlooked.

Reciprocal teaching is a useful strategy for parents to use when they are concerned about comprehension. Ideally, children will become independent with this approach and will eventually learn to monitor their comprehension. Until they are able to do that, however, it is important to put strategies in place that will get them to the point where they will automatically recognize they do not comprehend and know what to do about it. Reciprocal teaching forces them to recognize whether or not they understand what they are reading.

Parents too can use this type of approach by talking though the text or the pictures in the story with the child. For example they may ask the child 'What is happening in the picture?' or 'What do you think the story will be about from looking at the picture?'. Paired reading and shared reading can also be used by parents. Shared reading involves the parent reading a sentence and then the child reading a sentence.

Writing

There are some general points that can be made in relation to writing. Quite a number of students with dyslexia will have writing difficulties and there can be an overlap between dyslexia and dysgraphia (writing difficulties).

- Avoid using blank paper, it is a good idea to use lined paper with wide spacing.
- If the student has a significant handwriting difficulty then alternatives to handwriting can be considered.
- These include scribe, laptop, speech-to-text software, iPod/MP3 recorder/player. Digital voice recorders are useful and digital recording can be organized and downloaded onto the computer, or the student can type directly onto the computer.
- Mind maps can also be used either in planning prior to the written work or as a substitute for some types of written work.
- Keyboard skills – it is also a good idea to encourage the student to develop keyboard skills from as young an age as possible. Using the computer can be motivating and can provide some control over the learning process. 'All the Right Type' is one program which will aid in learning keyboarding: www.cnet.com.au/downloads/0,239030384,10 441206s,00.htm Free downloads are also available from www.brothersoft.com/downloads/all-the-right-type.html. The website www.shambles.net also has a considerable amount of really useful game activities for developing typing skills that can be appealing.

Creative writing (writing frames)

Quite often children and young people with dyslexia can be very creative in their ideas but have difficulty in putting these down on paper in a structured and organized manner. They may restrict their vocabulary and not show their full ability in the written piece. They may also have difficulty in developing their ideas in written work although they may be able to do this in discussion. One of the strategies that can promote expressive writing is writing frames.

A writing frame consists of a skeleton outline given to students to scaffold their non-fiction writing. This is essentially a framework that consists of a number of different key words or phrases and can form a template for the piece of writing. This is important for students with dyslexia as often they may have the ideas but have difficulty in putting them in a logical sequence and sometimes generating the information in the first place. Writing fames can act as a cue or prompt to help to generate the argument, particularly in non-fiction writing.

An example of a writing frame is shown below.

Argument

I think that _____ because _____.

The reasons for my thinking this are, firstly _____

another reason is _____.

Moreover _____ because _____.

These (facts / arguments / ideas) show that _____.

Some people think that _____ because

they argue that _____.

Discussion

Another group who agree with this point of view are _____.

They say that _____.

On the other hand _____

I disagree with the idea that_____.

They claim that _____

they also say _____.

My opinion is _____

because _____.

Source: Adapted from David Wrays website, www.warwick.ac.uk/staff/D.J.Wray/index.html.

Wray also advocates that teachers need to ensure that children are given adequate opportunities to acquire the requisite knowledge about themselves as writers, about the writing process and about the demands of particular writing tasks, including textual structures. They also need to ensure that this knowledge develops beyond simply knowing that certain things can be done in writing to knowing **how** they can be done, and **why** they should be done. Therefore the focus is on the process involved in the emerging and finished product rather than on the product itself.

Some strategies to help integrate metacognitive skills in the writing process include thinking aloud while writing and critically examining and revising writing decisions, for example asking themselves 'Why do I write this?', or 'Why did I explain something in this manner?'.

According to Wray, writers also need to anticipate potential difficulties, make judgements and reconciliations between competing ideas, as well as show an awareness of the needs of their potential and actual readership.

Brainstorming

Brainstorming is a good way to help students with dyslexia develop their vocabulary and provide outlets for creative thinking. It can be done as a whole-class activity, which is one key advantage. The student with dyslexia can often excel in this type of situation. When the brainstorming activity is finished, they should write a list of ideas to work from for writing. Try to get them to write a long list of at least 10 items.

It is important to note that spelling never counts in brainstorming activities and it is often a good idea to have someone scribing so the student with dyslexia can focus solely on getting the ideas out. It is a good idea to try to vary the activities by using a whiteboard or a chalkboard to get away from a regular lined piece of paper and pencil.

Choose a topic to brainstorm that will be of some interest to your student, such as:

- Uses for a stick
- Skateboard brand names
- Vacation destinations
- Things that are green
- Sports equipment
- Things to take to the beach
- Cars
- In a forest
- Types of dogs
- Musicians
- Favourite snack foods.

Source: Adapted from Reid, G. and Green, S. (2011), 100 Ideas for Supporting Pupils with Dyslexia.

Writing vocabulary

Often students with dyslexia require support to help them extend their writing vocabulary. They may have a good oral vocabulary but it may not be evident in writing. Developing a writing vocabulary can be achieved by providing them with a list of key words that they may want to use in a piece of writing. These words can be divided into different categories such as descriptive words, names, places, 'feeling' words. The use of cloze passages (passages with some words missing) can be a good exercise and the student can fill in the blanks from a list that is provided.

The creation of a personal word bank can also be useful. It is a good idea to have the meaning of the word next to the word to ensure that the student uses the word appropriately.

A good source book for developing creative writing skills is the book *How to Write Like a Writer* by Bob Hext from Crossbow Education (www.crossboweducation.com). This is an excellent resource on supporting writing. It is a user-friendly resource and it progresses to more challenging activities, so it will be useful for upper primary and secondary school.

Paired writing

The method 'paired writing', developed by Keith Topping may be also be useful. It provides a structured framework to support interactive collaborative behaviours through all stages of the writing process.

There is clear role division of labour at every stage, to modulate information processing, promote flow and reduce anxiety. The emphasis is on thinking, planning, intelligent questioning, self-disclosure and discussion, reorganisation and restructuring. In paired writing, partners offer a continuous sense of audience and almost immediate feedback. Paired writing works within behaviourist principles of constant inbuilt feedback and cross-checking to ensure that what is written makes sense to both partners in the process.

Step 1 involves 'ideas generation'. Step 2 is drafting. In Step 3 the pair looks at the text together while the helper reads the draft out loud with expression. Step 4 is editing. First the writer considers where he/she thinks improvements are necessary, marking this with a coloured pen, pencil or highlighter. In Step 5 the writer copies out a 'neat' or 'best' version and the final step involves evaluation. The pair should self-assess their own best copy.

Technical vocabulary

Often when students with dyslexia reach the secondary school stage they may have difficulty with the technical vocabulary in different subjects. They may for example confuse words that sound similar such as *mitosis* and *meiosis*. It is also a good idea to help them develop their own subject vocabulary book so they can note the word together with its meaning.

Spelling

Some strategies for spelling include the following:

- Use key words and visuals to reinforce spelling rules and concepts.
- Use mnemonics to help with recall of non-phonetic words.
- There are a number of useful computer programs that can also be helpful with spelling, making it a fun activity. The company www.spellingmadesimple.com have a good range of software for spelling.
- The School Zone Spelling 2 pack also has a range of fun activities in spelling (www.schoolzone.com).
- Cued spelling (Marlin 1997) can be useful – research conducted by Marlin found that cued spelling:
  - enabled pupils to develop less teacher-dependent methods for improving their spelling;
  - improved pupils' overall spelling at the same time as encouraging them to take risks and attempt to spell difficult words rather than giving up;
  - helped pupils identify their own learning style;

- promoted co-operative learning and led to increased confidence;
- encouraged pupils to use more descriptive language, continuing speech and qualifying phrases to aid description in their writing.

Marlin describes cued spelling as a method to aid the learning of spelling using collaborative cues or prompts, such as rhyme, word association and abbreviation. In the first instance teachers draw up spelling sheets with five columns containing different types of words. The cued spelling procedure involves ten steps and is displayed prominently, as are the different types of cues, so that children can refer to them easily. At the beginning of each week, children check which words on the list they can spell and ask their partner to give them a quick test. Every day from Monday to Thursday each child chooses one word from each column of the spelling sheet and writes it on their diary sheet. They use the ten steps and the cues to learn their five words each day. On Friday, partners review their 20 words from the week with a quick test. If any words are incorrectly spelt they repeat the procedure until they are spelt correctly.

Source: *www.ntrp.org.uk/sites/all/documents/Marlin%20-%20paired%20spelling%20-%2097.pdf.*

The ten steps that are widely used in cued spelling are:

1. Pupils select a word to learn or are given target words.
2. Pairs enter the words into their spelling diaries.
3. Pairs read the word together.
4. Speller and helper choose cues together.
5. Pairs repeat cues aloud.
6. Speller says cues while helper writes word.
7. Helper says cues while speller writes word.
8. Speller writes word quickly and says cues aloud.
9. Speller writes word quickly.
10. Speller reads word aloud.

Source: www.gtce.org.uk/tla/rft/phonics0707/phonics0707cs/casestudy4.

The programme called Paired Spelling is also particularly useful in eliminating ingrained and learnt spelling habits, which may result in habitual wrong spellings. Topping has been very influential in developing paired spelling procedures (Topping, 1996). He suggests that the design of paired spelling incorporates many of the features of paired reading. It should be carried out around three times a week for six weeks.

Memory

Students with dyslexia often have difficulties with working memory. This involves holding two or more pieces of information at the same time and usually carrying out a processing activity such as writing or counting. To deal with this it is a good idea to ensure that the student only gets one task at a time or one piece of information. It is also important to remember that students with dyslexia need overlearning. That means that they will need a great deal of repetition in order to consolidate a piece of new learning.

Long-term memory may also be a difficulty. A great deal of the challenges with long-term memory are in fact due to lack of overlearning. Additionally the student with dyslexia may have difficulty with organizing information and this can lead to the information not being consolidated.

Some suggestions for developing long-term memory include:

- Repetition – students with dyslexia need opportunities for repetition and as indicated above – overlearning.
- Prioritizing – this involves helping students decide what to do first and what is less important. This can apply to daily tasks as well as to specific areas of study. This can help to reduce the burden of remembering a lot of information at the same time.
- Organizing information – this is important for memory – the key to organizing information is to re-arrange the information so it can be more easily understood and retained. Students with dyslexia may benefit from using headings to help to organize information. Visuals can also re-enforce this. This helps to personalize the information and this is crucial for retention and recall.
- Mind Mapping© — mind maps are a good way to use visuals and also help the student with organization. Mind Maps can also show the relationship between different facts and concepts and therefore can help to give a deeper understanding of the subject and the connections between different aspects.
- Chunking is an excellent strategy for organizing information and can also to help with retention of information.

Connections

It is important that students with dyslexia are able to develop connections between different curricular areas and topics, as well as word families. This helps learning become more meaningful and aids understanding and the development of higher level concepts. Questions that students can ask that can help to develop connections include:

- Is there anything about the new learning that is familiar?
- What is familiar and why?
- How did I tackle this before?
- Should I do the same again, or can I improve on this?

This can help connect between previous and new learning which is helpful for developing concepts ideas and higher-order thinking skills.

Maths

There are a number of barriers that can prevent the student with dyslexia from achieving in maths. For example abstract concepts and ideas can be difficult for students with dyslexia as they require organization and access to knowledge, rules, techniques, skills and concepts.

Often the rules that play an important part in mathematics have to be rote-learned. Some other maths skills that may be difficult to access for students with dyslexia are the spatial skills that are needed to help understand shape, symmetry, size and quantity, and the linear skills that are needed to help understand sequence, order and the representations found in the number system.

These aspects can prove demanding for dyslexic students, and in addition they still have the literacy and other difficulties associated with dyslexia such as working memory, speed of processing and automaticity. These can all have some implications for mathematics.

The following factors can also contribute to the demands of mathematics for students with dyslexia.

- Linear and sequential processing.
- Sequencing and precision.
- Long-term memory and information retrieval.
- Working memory.

It is important that students with dyslexia are presented with small amounts of information at a time. Some strategies that may help with maths include the following:

- Using visual skills to learn challenging words that are commonly used in maths.
- Noting down each step of the maths investigation and the sequence of steps.
- Allowing extra time to ensure that there is not too much pressure and to ease the anxieties of maths.
- Giving instructions one step at a time.
- Teaching visualization and techniques such as highlighting, mnemonics and colour coding.
- Talking about the topic before the task to ensure that the student has understood the instructions.
- Encouraging the student to write down the mathematical symbol in the place where it is normally used and highlight it in colour.
- Make visual facts cards for the properties of different shapes.

There are a number of excellent websites with maths games such as www.sheppardsoftware.com/math.htm that provide fun and stimulating strategies for different types of maths activities.

Music

Some of the barriers that the student with dyslexia can experience include:

- The reading of music – this can be learning a new language. Students have to learn the meaning of symbols, some with only subtle differences between them, and know when and how to use them.
- Reading music requires visual, as well as memory skills and this can put some additional burden on the visual processing system. There is evidence that some students with dyslexia may have a degree of unstable vision relating to convergence difficulties, other difficulties relating to visual sensitivity and visual processing difficulties relating to the magnocellular visual system.

- The nature of music scores – lines are positioned close together, and visual blur may occur as well as omissions and additions due to eye-tracking difficulties; indeed, in some cases the lines in a music score may close up and appear distorted.
- Processing difficulties – students have to read the music score, reintepret it for the instrument and reproduce it in a different form in the instrument being played. There are at least three simultaneous tasks in that activity, and these will present some difficulties for the student with dyslexia and impose a burden on working memory. Additionally, these activities have to be carried out at some speed and processing speed difficulties are often characteristic of dyslexia.
- The student has to keep in time with other instruments in the orchestra and, perhaps, also watch the conductor. There are, therefore, considerable simultaneous processing activities occurring when the person with dyslexia is reading music and playing an instrument at the same time.
- Co-ordination difficulties can also affect the performance of the student.

Ditchfield (2001) provides suggestions for teachers that can easily be incorporated into everyday teaching:

- If a student forgets their music, or their instrument, it needs to be understood that this is very likely because they are dyslexic.
- It is often difficult for them to follow sequential instructions and to remember them. It may be useful for the teacher to have spare copies of music or an alternative lesson plan.
- Many musicians need to practise small sections carefully and repetitively. This may be particularly helpful for the dyslexic person who may take longer to learn it.

Dyslexia-friendly approaches to teaching

Many of the strategies used that can be described as dyslexia friendly will be helpful for all students. These are therefore ideal for the inclusive classroom.

Preparing text

It is important to ensure that the text is accessible for students with dyslexia. Some guidelines on modifying texts to reduce reading difficulty are shown below.

- Shorten sentences.
- Use easier, shorter, more familiar words. Cut out technical vocabulary, unless it is absolutely essential.
- Spread out the text so that it is less dense on the page.
- Simplify sentence structure.
- Turn passive verbs ('He was bitten by the dog') into active verbs ('The dog bit him').
- Give a step-by-step explanation of concepts.

Guidance for all teachers

Some other suggestions for dyslexia-friendly approaches are shown below.

- **Small steps** – it is important, especially since children with dyslexia may have short-term memory difficulties, to present tasks in small steps. In fact one task at a time is probably sufficient. If multiple tasks are specified then a checklist might be a useful way for the child to note and self-monitor his/her progress.
- **Group work** – It is important to plan for group work. The dynamics of the group is crucial and dyslexic children need to be in a group where at least one person in the group is able to impose some form of structure to the group tasks. This can act as a modelling experience for dyslexic children – it is also important that those in the group do not overpower the dyslexic child – so someone with the ability to facilitate the dyslexic child's contribution to the group is also important. This would make the dyslexic child feel they are contributing to the group. Even though they may not have the reading ability of the others in the group, they will almost certainly have the comprehension ability, so will be able to contribute if provided with opportunities.
- **Use of coloured paper** – there is some evidence that different colours of background and font can enhance some children's reading and attention.
- **Layout** – the page layout is very important and this should be visual but not overcrowded. A coloured background is also usually preferable. Font size can also be a key factor and this should not be too small. In relation to the actual font itself, it has been suggested that Sassoon font, Comic Sans and Times New Roman are among the most dyslexia-friendly fonts.
- **Allow** additional time – some dyslexic children will require a substantial amount of additional time, particularly for tasks like copying from the board and writing exercises.
- Produce a checklist to ensure instructions have been **understood**, such as: What is actually being said/asked? What is required of me? How will I know if I am right? Often dyslexic children do not get the right answer because they have not fully understood the task. Take time to ensure the task is fully understood before allowing the child to work independently.
- Put different types of information under different **headings**. This can help with long-term memory and the organization of information.
- Provide **key** words – this is crucial as often dyslexic children have difficulty in identifying key words. They may often go for the irrelevant aspects of a passage or provide too much information because they have difficulty in identifying the key points.
- Use **multi-sensory** techniques – visual, auditory, kinaesthetic and tactile. This is important as it ensures that at least some of the activities will be tapping into the child's strong modality (i.e. the child's learning preferences – his/her preferred mode of learning).
- Use **mnemonics** to boost memory – this can be fun as well as an effective means of learning. It is best to personalize the mnemonic by encouraging the child to develop his/her own mnemonic.
- Use of **ICT** to help with processing speed and learner independence. There are a vast number of excellent ICT programs that can boost all aspects of learning. Computer programs can also help with learner autonomy.
- Make sure **group dynamics** are right and constructive for the dyslexic student. This is important as group work can be very rewarding but only if the dyslexic child is in a

constructive group. Try to ensure the group has not too many children who do a lot of talking – groups need listeners too.

- Use **enquiry** approaches – to promote thinking skills. Problem-solving activities can be useful as often there is not too much reading before the problem can be tackled. Similarly with fact-finding tasks – these can also be motivating but ensure there is clear guidance on how to find the information. A child with dyslexia can waste a lot of time looking for information on the Internet or in the library and may gather irrelevant information. It is important therefore to provide a clear structure for this.

- Use **tape** recorders to allow them to record their thoughts. This can be good for helping with metacognition (that is being aware of how one learns). Recording their thoughts on a tape it promotes self-thinking. They need to be aware of how they are actually tackling a task to be able to record their thoughts and this process helps with metacognitive awareness.

- Look for ways of boosting the learner's **self-esteem**. It is important that children's self-esteem is continually being boosted as it will encourage them to take risks with learning where otherwise they may have given up. It is crucial therefore that tasks are designed to ensure the child will experience some success. It is through success that self-esteem is boosted and success comes if the task that is presented is achievable. That is why it is so important that the planning of tasks is given a high priority.

- Try to develop their ability to **question** and to ask the right kind of questions about the task. This is important because it helps the child to understand the task if they know the right kind of questions to ask. This can be quite difficult and it is important that this is practiced through pre-task discussion.

- **Highlight** photocopied text and use a dyslexia-friendly typeface. There are a number of different typefaces that can be seen as dyslexia friendly (see above) – but it may not be best for all dyslexic children so it is best to try a few different fonts and let the child decide what is the best.

- Ensure instructions are **short** and clear. It is best to provide a series of short tasks rather than one long one. This also makes it easier for children to monitor their own progress.

- Use **games** to consolidate vocabulary – game activities can be excellent for motivating students with dyslexia. Crossbow Education has an excellent range of games (www.crossboweducation.com). These include digital phonics, Spingoes phonics activities, Magic 'E' Spin it, Knockout, and Vowel Digraph Triplets

- Try to develop **creativity** and thinking and problem-solving skills. This is vitally important and is an area that is often overlooked when teaching dyslexic children because there is inclined to be a preoccupation with teaching literacy skills. It is crucial that the higher-order thinking skills are not overlooked and these need to be given a high priority.

- Subject glossary.

It is a good idea to incorporate a subject glossary into your dyslexia/learning difficulty-friendly approaches. This can consist of challenging words or concepts in different subjects and you can encourage students to develop their own glossary of terms. This can be added to from time to time and also illustrated to make it easier for them to understand and retain.

Motivation and effective learning

It is very easy for students with dyslexia to become de-motivated. Many of the strategies below can help all students, and they can certainly be used without drawing unnecessary attention to their difficulties.

Ten suggestions for motivation

1. Encourage diversity in learning styles

Children's learning patterns are often the result of how they were taught, the learning environment and ethos of the school. For some children this is perfectly satisfactory as their styles and preferences match those of the school. For others however this may not be the case and often students with dyslexia come into this category. For that reason it is important to encourage diversity in the classroom so that the student can opt for his/her own individual learning preference. This can be done by offering them choice and giving them the opportunity to utilize their own learning style in the classroom. Some factors that can be considered include school culture, school climate, teacher and parent expectations, teaching style and classroom norms and practices. It is therefore important to reflect on the above and ensure that flexibility is used to encourage diversity. In this way it is likely that the student with dyslexia will be accommodated.

2. Encourage creativity

It is interesting to reflect on the fact that many people with dyslexia develop their creativity after they leave school. Many fail at school, or certainly do not shine. This is because the examination system often does not encourage creativity. For many learners with dyslexia creativity is the principal motivating factor.

3. Ensure success with small achievable steps

Success is an essential factor for motivation and for effective learning. It is the teacher's responsibility to ensure that the learner meets with success. If success is not evident then the task has to be further differentiated. Most students learn new information in steps. This can be useful for students with dyslexia but often they have a holistic learning style. This means that they need to have an overview of the whole area first. It is a good idea to talk over the whole project or topic first so they have an overview and this will help them develop the individual parts.

4. Provide feedback to students about their own personal progress

Progress is personal – progress for one may not be progress for someone else. This is very true for students with dyslexia. It is important that the criteria for progress are not generalized but instead should be individualized. Once it is decided what exactly constitutes progress for the individual student this should be discussed and negotiated with the learner and then personal goals can be established and progress more easily identified. This can help the dyslexic student set his/her own achievable goals.

5. Learners need to believe in their own abilities

Self-belief is crucial if one is to accomplish any degree of success and motivation. Even those people with dyslexia who seem to have achieved a great deal of success – in the class, industry or in sport – may have a surprisingly low level of self-belief and need and rely on positive feedback to ensure they can believe in their own abilities. This can be because they are not receiving the positive feedback they need. The common perception might be that these people do not need it because they know they are successful. The key point here is not to take this for granted and not to assume that some successful learners do not need positive and continuous feedback and encouragement in order for them to develop and maintain self-belief. This is very important for the learner with dyslexia.

6. Acknowledge the individual styles of each person

This is important for students with dyslexia – even though it can be challenging in an inclusive classroom. But even if the young person is only made aware of his/her learning style, this can at least set them up for independent learning at home and beyond school. This awareness is important as it can help them take some responsibility for their own learning.

7. Use group work effectively

Working in groups can be a great motivator for students with dyslexia. They can often thrive in a group when they may struggle when working individually. At the same time it is important to ensure that the dynamics of the group provides a positive experience for the student with dyslexia and of course the other students in the group. It is too easy for one or several children to be passengers and feel 'left out' of a group and this may happen to the student with dyslexia. It might be an idea to pair the student with dyslexia with someone who can be encouraging and with whom he/she feels at ease.

8. Encourage self-assessment

This is important as it helps children with dyslexia take control of their own learning. They should be encouraged to assess their own progress and this can be a motivator in itself. The key point is that they should be able to decide what they want to achieve and the teacher's role in this is to guide and monitor their progress. Self-assessment encourages self-reflection and this helps to develop higher-order thinking skills.

9. Develop student responsibility

The key to successful learning is student autonomy. This is not always afforded students with dyslexia. Yet it is important as it provides the learner with some control over his/her learning. It is this control that fosters responsibility and makes it possible for the student with dyslexia to move from extrinsic to intrinsic motivation.

10. Focus on learning as well as teaching

It is important to identify and recognize the strengths shown by children with dyslexia and to attempt to incorporate these strengths into a teaching programme. Knowing about how children learn and how to make learning more effective through study skills and good teaching practices can be extremely beneficial for students with dyslexia. It is important to recognize the need to boost their self-esteem as it is too easy for them to become discouraged and lose interest in learning.

Creativity and learning styles

Dunn and Griggs (1988) suggested that seven learning style traits characterize high-risk students from others. These are:

- Need for mobility while learning.
- Requiring a variety of teaching and learning approaches and peer learning.
- Most productive learning time is late morning, afternoon or evening, but not early morning.
- An informal seating design for learning, not traditional desks and chairs.
- Low illumination.
- Tactual and kinaesthetic learning, certainly when first learning a new topic or skill.
- Multi-sensory teaching packages.

In a Canadian study Brodhead and Price (1993) found similar results to the United States in relation to studying the learning styles of creative students – they also preferred working in groups, preferred music, afternoon or evening learning and tactile and kinaesthetic learning. Indeed in a cross-cultural study of 'high-risk', creative students from seven countries – Brazil, Canada, Guatemala, Israel, Korea, The Philippines and the United States – Price and Milgram (1993) found many similarities, such as the need to learn kinaesthetically and self-motivation. There were differences such as the scope for creative activity and the researchers suggested that cultural factors influence the individual's creative activities. In general however the study did support the notion that creative students, particularly in relation to a specific domain, such as art, drama, literature, music and dance, do have significantly similar learning styles to each other but significantly different from other groups of students with different abilities.

Often people with dyslexia have relatively low self-esteem, and significantly this low self-esteem is not confined to only academic self-esteem. It can be concluded that there may be a number of risk factors in the lives of dyslexic people which can contribute to low self-esteem. Literacy is only one aspect of a much bigger picture and clearly low self-esteem (possibly accompanied by high anxiety) need to be considered as these factors can affect every aspect of the lives of dyslexic individuals.

Using technology in the classroom

Materials and teaching approaches for learners with dyslexia can be enriched through the use of computer programs. There are a number of companies that specialize in software for learners with dyslexia. One such company is iANSYST Ltd (www.dyslexic.com). They provide a full range of speech recognition and text-to-speech software using the more advanced RealSpeak® voices which are a significant improvement (with a much more human-sounding voice) on previous versions. Such software can be very helpful for proofreading as it is easier to hear mistakes than to see them and it can help to identify if any words are in the wrong place. iANSYST recommend software such as Wordsmith v2 as it can scan and edit paper-based text and images, listen to text being read back and can help the learner explore creative writing with speech support. The TextHELP® range is also highly recommended. TextHELP®-type and touch 4.0 includes the text help spellchecker which has been specifically developed for use by learners with dyslexia. Other technological support includes the Quicktionary Reading Pen that transfers words from the page to the LCD display when scanned by the pen. The package can be upgraded to extend its capabilities in order to convert it into a translator with over 20 different languages available. The reading pen also speaks the words and can define the word when requested. There are a number of typing tuition programs that can assist with the development of touch typing. These include the KAZ Typing Tutor which has an age range of 7–adult and First Keys to Literacy which has a recommended age range of 5–9 years. Some of the keyboarding activities include word lists, individual letter recognition, digraphs and rhymes, and picture, letter and word prompts. There is also a program called Magictype, which is a fun interactive program for the 6–11 age range.

There are other popular programs that help to organize information, such as Kidspiration for the 5–11 age range, and Inspiration, which is also suitable for adults. These help to develop ideas and concepts with examples of concept maps and templates that incorporate a range of subject areas, such as languages, arts, science and social studies.

R-E-M software produce computer materials specifically designed for dyslexia and have produced a catalogue specifically on dyslexia (www.r-e-m.co.uk). A considerable range can also be found on the Educators' Publishing Service website (www.epsbooks.com).

How dyslexia affects children's learning

Learning is a process and this process can be described as dynamic. This means that different parts of the brain interact with other parts and each relies on and interacts with the other. For example the various parts of the brain that deal with visual/auditory/memory/understanding/co-ordination may all be used simultaneously to tackle a task. It is often this simultaneous use of learning skills that is challenging for children with dyslexia. For that reason tasks need to be structured, clarified and preferably focused towards the student's stronger areas of learning. Children with dyslexia are usually stronger visually or kinaesthetically, as opposed to auditorily. That means initial learning will be more meaningful if presented visually or through the experience of learning (kinaesthetics).

Kinaesthetic experiences can be helpful to reinforce learning. Kinaesthetic means experiencing learning. Activities that involve drama and role playing, or investigation and enquiry activities, such as in a survey, interview or questionnaire, all utilize kinaesthetic skills. Each of these activities involves experiential learning.

Cognition

Cognition is important for learning. It describes the actual processes involved in learning a piece of information. This relates to memory, understanding, organizing and generally making sense of information. Often children with dyslexia have what can be described as cognitive difficulties. These include memory and organizing information, and often can be quite serious difficulties that the dyslexic child needs to overcome for effective learning.

What is important however is that good teaching can help to overcome all of these cognitive difficulties. Much can be done to aid the child's memory, and assistance by the teacher to help the dyslexic child organize information can help him/her learn more effectively. The teacher can play a key role therefore in helping dyslexic children overcome cognitive difficulties.

Metacognition

Cognition, as indicated above, means learning, metacognition means learning to learn. This implies that children can be taught to be more effective learners. This is very important for dyslexic children. The research indicates that children with dyslexia may be weak in metacognitive awareness and therefore have difficulty in knowing how to go about tackling a problem. This means they may not be sure on **how** to, for example, interpret a question or to work out the most efficient way of answering it, or in fact to remember any piece of information. The development of metacognitive skills can be aided by programmes that are essentially 'study skills' programmes. Often study skills are seen to be part of examination preparation, but in fact this is calling on the skill too late. Study skills, particularly for learners with dyslexia, should be provided as young as possible. Becoming efficient in studying and learning helps the learner make connections between different pieces of information and this can help with transfer of learning and generally more efficient use of information.

Metacognition is not a new idea. Vygotsky (1962) suggested that there are two stages in the development of knowledge: first, its automatic unconscious acquisition and second, a gradual increase in active conscious control over that knowledge. It is important therefore that students with dyslexia obtain control over the learning process.

The strategy known as 'KWL' can help with this and can be used for reading and for studying text in different curricular subjects. The letters KWL represent three steps in the process. This strategy is suitable for all age groups and the first two steps are gone through before reading the text.

K: What do I **know** already in this area? The student reflects on what they know already and can state it orally or write it down.

W: What do I **want** to find out? Each student thinks of what they expect to get from the reading. They may write it down or express it verbally.

L: What have I **learned**? Students read the text silently and say or write what they have learned from the reading.

This is essentially a metacognitive approach because it encourages the learner to reflect on their own learning. This is essential in order to gain self-knowledge and independence in learning.

Self-esteem

Self-esteem is important for learning. A child will learn more effectively and will be more motivated to learn if his/her self-esteem is high. This is also very important for learners with dyslexia. Young children with dyslexia realize very soon after commencing formal education that some aspects of school education, such as reading, spelling and writing, are challenging for them. This can result in feelings of failure and frustration. It can lower the child's motivation and self-esteem in relation to learning. Effort needs to be made to ensure children with dyslexia are provided with opportunities to gain some success, as it is only through success that self-esteem will be enhanced. Activities such as circle time (Mosley 1996) can help to provide opportunities for enhancement of self-esteem.

How the teacher and the school can help

Many of the points mentioned above will benefit all learners. This is important as it indicates that good and effective teaching practices will greatly aid children with dyslexia without the necessity of having to resort to expensive commercially produced programmes. It is certainly important to know about these programmes and it is also important to appreciate the characteristics of dyslexia and to recognize that children with dyslexia need to be seen as individuals as each child may show different characteristics to varying degrees.

Communication

One of the important issues in dealing with dyslexia is that of communication. Often the controversy and confusion that can exist in the field of dyslexia result from a breakdown in effective communication between the school and the home. There are many conflicting views on how dyslexia can be dealt with. Some of these conflicting views emerge from information on commercial websites and other types of uncontrolled and often untested commercial outlets. It is important that the school should be able to advise on the suitability of programmes for dyslexic children. This can be done by assuring parents that the best is being done for their child. This can be achieved through the school communicating with parents effectively. This means informing parents how the school has recognized the dyslexic characteristics of the child and how they are meeting his/her needs. It is important to reassure parents that the school does take dyslexia seriously; otherwise parents will be swayed by persuasive commercially orientated programmes that claim unrivalled successes. It is useful if the school has a member of staff who has undertaken training in dyslexia, as this person can provide information to parents on any new programme that they may have seen advertized on the web or elsewhere.

Strategies for curriculum access

Below are some strategies that can be used to help the student with dyslexia overcome the barriers that may prevent curriculum access.

- Talk – discussion is crucial for most children with dyslexia. It is an active form of learning and can also help the teacher monitor the child's understanding. It can be used in both learning and assessment.
- Drama – some learners can develop comprehension more effectively through active participation. This uses the kinaesthetic (experiential) modality and this type of learning can be essential for some learners.
- Drawing – visual representation can be also be essential for many learners with dyslexia, some of whom can only learn visually, so even the most basic of information may have to be presented visually.
- Listening – all learners need to develop listening skills, and for some this can be challenging. It is important that listening is given a high priority – but it is equally important that listening should be only for short periods of time and interspersed with other forms of learning, particularly discussion.

- Role play – one of the key points about developing learning skills is that it learning should be personalized by the learner. This will make learning more meaningful and will help to develop comprehension skills. One way of achieving this is to develop imagination. Role play can be an excellent tool for developing imagination. It helps to facilitate children's creativity and furthermore can make learning individual. Additionally role play uses the kinaesthetic modality and this experiential type of learning can benefit many learners.

This chapter has provided a range of strategies that can essentially be incorporated into whole-class intervention. Although not all may not be seen as specialized and focused exclusively on students with dyslexia, they can be effective. Furthermore they can also be inclusive. It is important that students with dyslexia feel that they 'fit in' – that the learning environment is one that appeals to them, and makes them feel comfortable and motivated to learn. For that reason it is important that classroom teachers as well as being familiar with these general whole-class approaches also need to have an understanding of what dyslexia is and how the student with dyslexia can deal with the barriers they may experience in the classroom. That is not to say that the individual needs of the student are not important – they are and this will be discussed in the next chapter on individual approaches and differentiation.

6 Supporting the learner: practical approaches and further considerations

Interventions and dyslexia

There is an ongoing and long-standing debate on the nature and purpose of specialist provision for dyslexia. Norwich and Lewis (2005) question the specialist approach that is often advocated for specialist categories such as dyslexia. Norwich (2009) also questions whether dyslexia is compatible with the principles of inclusive education. He suggests that some might argue that they each belong to conflicting perspectives (i.e. specialised approaches for dyslexia and inclusion are incompatible). He argues for a concept of *flexible interacting continua of provision* which differs from the conventional placement continuum of special provision. He argues that there are dangers of working at the disability-specific level and that even the 'dyslexia-friendly' movement is too narrow to enhance school provision. He suggests that educational provision has to balance *common* with *differentiated* provision so it can provide for individual needs in equitable and shared ways.

While it is recognised that there are individual differences among all students and also within sub-groups such as dyslexia, there is still a very strong body of opinion, and research evidence, to support the specialist approach. Pumfrey and Reason (1992) recognise the potential difficulties in evaluating pedagogical approaches for dyslexia when they suggest that 'the key issue is whether the considerable range of teaching/learning methods, techniques and materials available are differentially effective with pupils (who have) identifiably different learning characteristics' (p. 113). They also suggest that one of the important aspects of pedagogical approaches for children with dyslexia is the quality of teaching and that 'one important aspect of teaching quality is the knowledge, ability and willingness to look critically at the evidence … in support of particular methods' (p. 125). The view held by Pumfrey and Reason still holds good today – they suggest that for conceptual reasons there is unlikely ever to be a panacea for dyslexia. This view is supported by the comments made in the BPS (1999) working party report into Dyslexia and Psychological Assessment when it suggests that no fewer than ten different hypotheses can be associated with dyslexia. This indicates that we need to be open to a wider and more diverse view of dyslexia as there can be a wide range of characteristics associated with dyslexia which will in turn mean a broader range of teaching approaches should be considered.

The specialist position

The specialist position is strongly advocated by Dyslexia Action Training and Professional Development, http://training.dyslexiaaction.org.uk, a leading provider of specialist and short courses in the field of Dyslexia and Specific Learning Difficulties. Dyslexia Action has a range of specialist courses at all levels – school training, postgraduate training and ongoing professional development courses for teachers and other professionals as well as courses for parents. They receive support from the Training and Development Agency for Schools (TDA) in the UK. This is the national agency and recognised sector body responsible for training and development of the school workforce. There is therefore government acknowledgement of the need to develop specialist training in dyslexia. This was backed up by the Rose Review in the UK (2009). Rack (2010) indicates that in the Rose Review dyslexia is recognised as a central concern for all teachers and there is an emphasis on developing teachers' roles in identification and in the provision of support within the mainstream school. There is therefore an emphasis on equipping teachers to deal with dyslexia within an inclusive teaching situation. This represented a move from highly specialized individualised approaches (www.dyslexiaaction.org.uk/News/dr-john-racks-summary-of-the-rose-review).

The report does emphasise the importance of systematic phonically based teaching and the fact that there will be some children who will need long-term specialised input. Rack also indicates that the report calls for action to increase skills and knowledge for class teachers and to train more specialist teachers who play a key role in developing, delivering and evaluating educational interventions, especially for children with dyslexia. There is therefore a consensus that both mainstream and specialised approaches are necessary to support the broad range of children with dyslexia given the individual differences.

Nevertheless, given this debate it may be more productive to identify specific approaches by examining the barriers to learning experienced by the child. This would imply that each child is individual and the specific barriers may be different for different children. One way to deal with this is through the use of individual education plans (IEPs). These can identify the barriers to learning and identify strategies and approaches to overcome these barriers and contextualise them within the learning and the classroom situation.

Individual education plans (IEPs) – implications for children with dyslexia

Individual education plans can provide a means of ensuring the needs of children are met within the educational setting. The term 'individual education plan' can be used to refer to both the process of planning the next steps in a pupil's learning programme on the basis of an analysis of pupil needs, and the summative document used to record the IEP. In the Republic of Ireland, this is also referred to as the Individual Profile and Learning Programme. But in most countries, including the USA and Canada, the IEP has a specific purpose and is associated with some form of specialist input.

Individual education plans (IEPs) – contents *(see sample proforma opposite)*

IEPs can be invaluable and can provide both day-to-day information on specific performances, as well as medium- and long-term targets. It is also useful for parents as they can see the progress that is being made as well as the aims of the intervention.

In order for an IEP to be used appropriately it should contain at least the following:

- Details of the nature of the child's learning difficulties.
- The special educational provision to be made.
- Strategies to be used.
- Specific programmes, activities, materials.
- Any specialised equipment.
- Targets to be achieved.
- Time frame for any specified targets.
- Monitoring and assessment arrangements.
- Review arrangements with dates.

INDIVIDUAL EDUCATION PLAN

(Courtesy of the Lighthouse School, Cairo)

Name: _____

DoB: _____   Class: _____   Date: _____

	Medical Issues:
Strengths: (curricular, extra-curricular and preferred learning styles)	
Individual Learning Style/Preferences: **Social:** (Interaction/Communication/Learning with self/pair/peer/adult/Authority/Variety)	
Environmental: (Mobility/Food/Time of day/Light/Temp/Sound/Seating design)	
Emotional: (Motivation/Conformity/Persistence/Responsibility/Structure)	
Cognitive: (Instruction preference (Visual/Tactile/Auditory/Kinaesthetic)/Sequential,Simultaneous learning/Impulsive,Reflective/ Analytic,Global)	
Metacognition: (Resource & Environmental Choices/Self-Assessment/Prediction/Feedback)	
Areas to be developed: (targets should address these needs)	1:1 Programmes currently undertaken:
Suggestions from Psych-Ed evaluations:	

Targets:

Long-term Targets (to be achieved within the school year)	
Medium-term Targets (to be achieved by end of term set)	
Short-term Targets (to be achieved by end of month set)	
Strategies and Resources	
Provision – Who and When?	
Monitoring/ Success Criteria	
Monthly Review:	

Monthly Review:	Monthly Review:	Monthly Review:	End of Term Review:	Pupil's contribution and views:	Summary evaluation and future action – successful strategies, progress, concerns, issues, next steps, etc.

Signed:

Date:

It is important that the IEP is agreed by the parents, and the student, if appropriate, should also be involved in the discussions. An IEP should contain details of the students' strengths as well as the areas to be developed. A Personal Learning Plan should be developed from an IEP. This is really for the student's use and should contain the short-term learning targets, how these will be reached and a column to help the student monitor the progress towards achieving these targets.

Some other factors that can inform the development of a learning plan

- **Knowledge of the child's strengths and difficulties** – this is essential especially since not all children with dyslexia will display the same profile. This is therefore the best starting point as often strengths can be used to help deal with the weaknesses.

    For example, dyslexic children often have a preference for visual and kinaesthetic learning and a difficulty with auditory learning. Therefore phonics which relies heavily on sounds, and therefore the auditory modality, needs to be introduced together with visual and experiential forms of learning. The tactile modality involving touch and feeling the shape of letters that make specific words should also be utilised, as well as the visual symbol of these letters and letter/sound combinations.

- **Consultation** – the responsibility for dealing with children with dyslexia within the classroom should not solely rest with the class teacher. Ideally it should be seen as a whole-school responsibility. This means that consultation with school management and other colleagues is important, and equally it is important that time is allocated for this. Information from previous teachers, support staff, school management and parents are all important. Such joint liaison can help to ensure the necessary collaboration to provide support for the class teacher. Importantly this should be built into the school procedures and not be a reaction to a problem that has occurred – such collaboration can therefore be seen as preventative and proactive.

- **Current level of literacy acquisition** – an accurate and full assessment of the child's current level of attainments is necessary in order to effectively plan a programme of learning. The assessment should include listening comprehension as well as reading accuracy and fluency. Listening comprehension can often be a more accurate guide to the abilities and understanding of dyslexic children than reading and spelling accuracy. Indeed it is often the discrepancy between listening comprehension and reading accuracy that can be a key factor in identifying dyslexia. Information on the level of attainments will be an instrumental factor in planning for differentiation.

- **Cultural factors (bilingual students)** – background knowledge, particularly cultural factors, are important as these can influence the selection of books and whether some of the concepts in the text need to be singled out for additional and differentiated explanation. Cultural values are an important factor. It has been suggested that the 'big dip' in performance noted in some bilingual children in later primary school may be explained by a failure of professionals to understand and appreciate the cultural values, and the actual level of competence of the bilingual child, particularly in relation to conceptual development and competence in thinking skills. It is possible for teachers to misinterpret bilingual children's development of good phonic skills in the early stages of literacy development in English and they may in fact fail to note the difficulties that these children might be having with comprehension. When the difficulties later emerge, these children can be grouped inappropriately with native-speakers of English, have the more conventional problems with phonic awareness, or their difficulties are assumed to derive from specific perceptual problems rather than from the cultural unfamiliarity of the text.

In order for a teaching approach with bilingual students to be fully effective it must be comprehensive, which means that it needs to incorporate the views of parents and the community. This requires considerable preparation and pre-planning, as well as consultation with parents and community organizations.

Curriculum issues

Ideally all intervention should be integrated in some way into the curriculum. This transfer from specialized input to the main body of the curriculum is very important.
   Curriculum-based intervention can present two difficulties.

1.   Development of strategies to help the student cope with his/her dyslexic difficulties.
2.   Recognition of the difficulties in accessing the curriculum that can place the student with dyslexia at a disadvantage. This can be minimized through the use of accommodations.

It may only take some minor adjustments in planning and teaching to make a difference. Some accommodations can include:

- Additional time being provided to complete a task.
- Printed handouts being provided.
- Summaries of the work.
- Students working together in small groups.
- Marking and grading that is constructive.
- Work judged for content not spelling.

Differentiation

Differentiation is the vehicle by which teachers can help students with dyslexia access the full curriculum. This can be achieved in four ways:

1.   Differentiation by task.
2.   Differentiation by outcome.
3.   Differentiation by resources.
4.   Differentiation through support.

Differentiation by task and resources

These can be linked together but it is important to understand that differentiation does not only mean using a wider range of resources. Resources can support differentiated material and should be seen as supplementary.

Differentiation by task/resources involves the process of adapting materials to suit a range of learners' abilities and levels of attainment.

How this can be achieved will depend on the students' individual learning needs. Some suggestions include:

- **Abridged books**: these are books that have been condensed or shortened. The language is simplified and some of the information that could be considered unnecessary is taken out. In a non-fiction text the abridged version would summarize the main points as briefly as possible.
- **Abridged workbooks:** these are often available to accompany a novel study. It is important to ensure the workbooks are still challenging to the individual student.
- **Taped books:** Abridgement can also be a book that has been adapted into an audio version to use as a companion with the original version. Audio books are often available in both an abridged version and an unabridged version. The unabridged version is good if a student has poor reading skills but wants to follow along with the text or wants to appreciate the book in its entirety. This can be extremely beneficial in helping to develop the child's language experience and extending their vocabulary as well as providing an insight into narrative and story plots. The abridged version is good for simply following the storyline and will of course be much quicker to finish.

Presentation of material

Differentiation also includes how the material is presented. For example:

- **Font** – retyping in a larger, more dyslexic-friendly font such as Century Gothic (or those suggested in Chapter 5) can make it easier for students to read.
- **Paper** – use a different colour paper or different colour font. Some students are distracted by the glare off of white paper.
- **Key points** – provide a list of key points using bullets.
- **Heading and subheadings** – the organizational structure can make it much easier for a dyslexic student to read and understand.
- **Visual aids** – mind maps, spider grams, graphic organizers.
- **Key words or phrases** – these can be highlighted.
- **Quantity** – Smaller amounts of information broken down in order to present it in smaller amounts.

Accessibility of the task/content – in order to make the task accessible to the learner it may be necessary to:

- Reword the directions or instructions with simple vocabulary, and clear and short sentences in a logical sequential order. Keep the concept and ideas the same but change the vocabulary to be more easily understood.
- Read instructions, one step at a time, to the student.
- Adapt the task to fit the strengths of the student.
- Graduate the task from simple to more complex.
- Vary the activities or learning strategies to give the student alternatives to explore the content. For example they may use graphs or webs to show their comprehension of the concepts rather than writing a paragraph.

- Focus on the content of their writing rather than the spelling, punctuation and grammar.
- Use a picture dictionary – for some students a picture dictionary using colour where or when it is appropriate can be very useful. They can also personalise this.

Differentiation: some points to consider when planning a novel study
- Curriculum – how does the novel relate to the curriculum?
- Link the novel to background knowledge to enhance comprehension.
- Personal interests – is the student interested in the characters or the plot in the novel?
- Taped books – is the novel available in a taped version?
- Movie – has the novel been made into a movie? For some students it is very helpful to see the movie before reading the novel.
- Sequence events by chapter, event or by beginning, middle and end. This can be done by using a mind map, an organized chart, or drawings representing each chapter or event in sequential order.
- Use character webs listing characteristics of major and/or minor characters.

Differentiation using multi-sensory teaching

Use all the learning pathways in the brain: visual, auditory, tactile, kinaesthetic.

Ensure the tasks involve active learning. For example tracking while reading, asking questions during reading passages, tracing over letters or words.

Change positions, try sitting on a ball, standing on a balance board, writing on a whiteboard, lying on the floor, reading in beanbag chairs or on cushions on the floor.

Play games to reinforce concepts.

Differentiation by outcome

The following could be considered.

Opportunities to talk and discuss in the classroom. This can allow students to engage in 'print-free' debate and utilise their strengths in oral discussion. Talking about issues can help students develop logical thinking skills and reflect and elaborate on their understanding. This can be useful for students with dyslexia. Additionally, practice in discussion can also have an impact on the pupil's ability to question, infer, deduce, propose and evaluate.

Differentiation is not only about making classwork and printed material more accessible for students with dyslexia; it is also about making the assessment more appropriate and effective.

It can be argued that traditional forms of assessment can disadvantage the dyslexic student because usually there is a discrepancy (and this may be a significant discrepancy) between their understanding of a topic and how they are able to display that understanding in written form. This may be overcome through continuous and portfolio assessment in most subject areas.

The form overleaf can help the student develop self assessment.

MY PERSONAL LEARNING PLAN

(Courtesy of the Lighthouse School, Cairo)

Name:	Class:	Date:

I am good at:

I learn best by.....

I like to work.....

I like the room I am learning in to be.....

I need instructions to be...

I am motivated by.....

I know that I learn best using....

Start Date:			Review Date:	
Short-term Learning Targets	**How will I know when I have reached my target?**		**How am I doing?**	

What did I do well?

What do I need to do next?

Differentiation through support

It does need to be acknowledged that some children with dyslexia will need a teaching assistant or some form of additional support. The range of duties and responsibilities of teaching assistants vary considerably from school to school and country to country. Some have considerable responsibility and are involved in planning and assessment as well as in the teaching and learning process. Others may have little or no responsibility and carry out prescribed tasks. Irrespective of the role of teaching assistants they are in a key position to form a close interaction with children and to obtain a good understanding of children's needs. Some children with dyslexia will have access to teaching assistants and it is important that teaching assistants are familiar with dyslexia and have an understanding of the needs of students with dyslexia. There will be training implications here and it is crucial that teaching assistants are an integral part of school professional development courses.

A major evaluation of the role of teaching assistants in the UK conducted by HMI in the UK, (*Teaching assistants in primary schools: an evaluation of the quality and impact of their work,* Ofsted, April 2002, HMI 434) shows that teaching assistants in primary schools have played an important part in the implementation of the National Literacy and Numeracy Strategies by providing support to both teachers and pupils in the classroom. The report suggests that teaching assistants also played a key role in the intervention and catch-up programmes such as early literacy support and additional literacy support.

Metacognitive assessment

This can also be used as an alternative when differentiating outcomes and encourages students to think about the processes of learning in more detail. The deficit may not lie with the student with dyslexia, but with an assessment process that is unable to accommodate the diversity of learners. It is strongly advocated, therefore, that both teaching and assessment should be differentiated and diversified. This can be achieved through use of the multiple intelligence paradigm, which avails itself of Gardner's 'eight intelligences' (1999). This includes formal speech, journal-keeping, creative writing, poetry, verbal debate and storytelling as a means of assessing the verbal–linguistic modality. While we are still a long way from a dynamic assessment paradigm that focuses on metacognitive strategies and views assessment as a teaching rather than a testing tool, such assessment is reported as being used in some classroom contexts. Metacognitive assessment can be informative, as it can provide information about children's actual levels of understanding and can be used to develop the most effective teaching approaches for students, which can strengthen the link between assessment and teaching.

Subject differentiation

Some selected examples from different subjects (see also Chapter 5 on maths and music and later in this chapter with reference to secondary school subjects).

Mathematics

Barriers

Abstract concepts and ideas can be difficult for students with dyslexia. They require organisation and access to knowledge, rules, techniques, skills and concepts. Often, rules that play an important part in mathematics have to be rote-learned. Other skills that may be difficult to access for students with dyslexia are the spatial skills that are needed to help understand shape, symmetry, size and quantity, and linear skills that are needed to help understand sequence, order and the representations found in the number system.

These aspects can prove demanding for dyslexic students, and in addition they still have the literacy and other difficulties associated with dyslexia such as working memory, speed of processing and automaticity. These can all have some implications for mathematics.

They may understand the meaning of words such as 'difference', 'evaluate', 'odd', 'mean' and 'product', but then find that they have a quite different meaning in the context of mathematics.

The following factors can also contribute to the demands of mathematics for students with dyslexia:

- Linear and sequential processing (this can be demanding because dyslexic students usually have some difficulty with order and sequencing and yet in some mathematical problems logic and sequence are crucial in order to obtain the correct response).
- Precision is also necessary; and accuracy and detail because dyslexic people tend to be more global and random in their thinking.
- Long-term memory and information retrieval can be problematic for students with dyslexia.
- Much of this is due to the lack of organization at the cognitive level – that is, at the initial stage of learning. If learning is not organized at this crucial initial stage then retrieval will be difficult at a later stage.
- Students with dyslexia may therefore have some difficulty with effective storage as well as accessing and retrieving information. It is for that reason that learning styles in mathematics is important. Assisting a student to utilize a preferred learning style can help effective storage, retrieval and access to information.
- Working memory can also present some difficulties because it implies that students need to hold information in their short-term store, which could be a fraction of a second, and process that information into meaningful stimuli. This is very important in mathematics as mental operations are necessary to do this, which can be demanding for students with dyslexia, especially if information is presented in large chunks.

Music

Barriers

- The reading of music can relate to learning a new language. Students have to learn the meaning of symbols, some with only subtle differences between them, and know when and how to use them.

- Reading music requires visual, as well as memory skills and this can put some additional burden on the visual processing system. There is evidence that some students with dyslexia may have a degree of unstable vision relating to convergence difficulties, other difficulties relating to visual sensitivity and visual processing difficulties relating to the magnocellular visual system.
- The nature of music scores – lines are positioned close together, and visual blur may occur as well as omissions and additions due to eye-tracking difficulties; indeed, in some cases the lines in a music score may close up and appear distorted.
- Processing difficulties – students have to read the music score, re-intepret it for the instrument and reproduce it in a different form in the instrument being played. There are at least three simultaneous tasks in that activity, and these will present some difficulties for the student with dyslexia and impose a burden on working memory.
- The student has to keep in time with other instruments in the orchestra and, perhaps, also watch the conductor.
- Co-ordination difficulties can also affect the performance of the student.

Information processing: strategies for support

Dyslexia can be seen as a difference in how information is processed. It is important to identify strategies that can support the student at different stages of the information processing cycle. The stages of the information-processing cycle can relate to input, cognition and output.

Students with dyslexia may experience difficulties at any, or each, of these stages. Some suggestions for practical strategies for dealing with each of these stages include the following.

Input

- Present information in small units.
- Support to monitor comprehension – this can also involve encouraging self-questioning, particularly for students further up the school.
- For example:
  - What have I got to do here?
  - Do I understand the task?
  - What is my plan for completing this reading/task?
  - What do I already know about this topic?
  - How am I doing?
  - Do I need any more information?
  - Can I summarize, in my own words, what I have read?

Ensure overlearning takes place. Vary the range of materials and strategies.

These points above can help to ensure that the information is being processed by the student.

Cognition

This is the thinking and the reasoning stage. It is important to do the following:

- Encourage organizational strategies to help the student learn more efficiently.
- Help the student organize new material to be learned into meaningful chunks or categories.
- Relate the new information to previous knowledge to ensure that concepts are clearly understood.
- Place the information into a meaningful framework.
- Help the student develop specific memory strategies, such as Mind Mapping© and mnemonics.

Output: presentation

It is important to help the student pay careful attention to presentation. This can be done by doing the following:

- Using headings and subheadings in written work as this will help with structure.
- Encouraging the use of summaries in order to identify the key points.
- Monitoring and assessing learning at each point in the process.

It is worth recognizing at this point that the impact of dyslexia can be minimized for the learner if the teaching, assessment and presentation of the curriculum acknowledges these potential cognitive difficulties.

Teaching – principles

Multi-sensory

There are a considerable number of intervention strategies for teaching reading and spelling to children with dyslexia. Many of these incorporate elements of what can be described as good teaching and are normally of a multisensory nature. That is, they incorporate visual, auditory, kinaesthetic and tactile elements. This is important as dyslexic children often have difficulty receiving information using the auditory modality and it is crucial to ensure that they receive teaching input through their stronger modalities – these are usually the visual and kinaesthetic modalities. Kinaesthetic activities in particular are important as these imply that the learner is experiencing learning – this can be through drama, poetry or field trips and excursions, but it is important that the 'experience' is evident and the learner needs to be active and participatory throughout this experience.

Overlearning

Students with dyslexia also require considerable overlearning. This does not mean pure repetition of teaching through repetitive rehearsal, but rather the use of a range of teaching approaches to ensure that the same words or skills are being taught in different situations. If a new word is to be learnt then it is important that the new word is used in other contexts and the connections are deliberately made and that they are made clear to the learner. This also applies to spelling rules. Many spelling patterns can lend themselves quite easily to overlearning through the use of the pattern in different words. A word of caution: overlearning is not the same as rote repetition! It is important to be creative and to present the same learning objective through a variety of teaching approaches.

Automaticity

One of the reasons why overlearning is an important element is that children with dyslexia often take longer than some other children to achieve automaticity. The term 'automaticity' refers to the consolidation of skills that learners normally achieve through practice. It is suggested that children with dyslexia take a longer period of time and require more varied input than some other children to acquire automaticity. This can become clear when after a period of teaching a particular word or skill, the learner may still not have acquired mastery in that skill. This can be particularly the case if there is a break such as a holiday or even the weekend, when the word and the skills associated with the word have not been used. This is one of the reasons why dyslexic children need a considerable amount of practice in reading, including material that is below their current reading level. Reading material below their level will ensure some practice in reading, and help with automaticity, and reading material above their level will help to provide the development of comprehension and strategies associated with context and comprehension as well as the use of inferential strategies. This can also help the individual with dyslexia become more efficient at predicting and using inferences – these skills are necessary for comprehension, especially if the reader has a low level of decoding skills.

Structure

It is important that all learning experiences should be structured to meet the needs of children with dyslexia within the classroom situation. This is particularly important in a piece of writing. Some support using for example writing frames can provide an excellent structure guiding the student on the content of the beginning, middle and end of the writing piece. (see www.warwick.ac.uk/staff/D.J.Wray/ideas.html for good examples of these.

Students with dyslexia need a structure since some skills may not be learnt automatically and often these need to be explicitly taught.

Practice

There is also a strong view that phonically based programmes are the most appropriate for dyslexic children. This, however, needs to be considered in the light of the individual child's learning and literacy needs and these may vary for different children.

Game-type activities can be extremely helpful in both engaging the learner and also ensuring that the necessary phonically based element is included (see www. crossboweducation.com for examples of these).

Reid (2009) discusses many programmes that can be used for children with dyslexia, but it is important to note here that those that are specialised are not necessarily the most appropriate in the classroom situation. Many of the individualized approaches are essentially one-to-one approaches and often require some specialized training. For that reason the support approaches described in this chapter can be appropriate for the classroom teacher.

High-interest books

The *Hi-Lo readers* from LDA, Cambridge and other similar books such as those from Barrington Stoke (www.barringtonstoke.co.uk) can be beneficial in relation to motivation. These books, particularly those from Barrington Stoke, have been written with the reluctant reader in mind and can help children with dyslexia with reading fluency and also help in the development of reading comprehension and reading speed.

Creative writing

Creative writing can, in fact, be one of the strengths displayed by dyslexic children. Often, of course, it is not. They may show difficulties with structure, sequencing the story, putting their point across and general grammar, syntax and punctuation.

It is important, therefore, to ensure that dyslexic children are provided with a clear structure so they know **how** they may embark on the task. They may know a great deal of detail about the topic they are writing on, but the difficulties associated with structure and also word retrieval can lead to a stilted and less elaborate account that will not reflect their actual level of knowledge of the topic.

Examples of software to support literacy

textHELP®

The program known as textHELP® is particularly useful for assisting with writing and is discussed more fully at Chapters 2 and 5.

Kidspiration/Inspiration(www.inspiration.com)/Kidspiration

Kidspiration/Inspiration are software programs that help the learner develop ideas and organize thinking. Through the use of diagrams the student is helped to comprehend words, concepts and information. Essentially the use of diagrams can help with the creating and modifying of concept maps and makes the organization of ideas easier. Learners can also prioritise and rearrange their ideas. These programs can, therefore, be used for brainstorming, organizing, pre-writing, concept mapping, planning and outlining. In Inspiration, which is for age 9–adult (Kidspiration is for children below 9), there are 35 inbuilt templates and these can be used for a range of subjects, including English, history and science. Dyslexic individuals often think in pictures rather than words. This technique can be used for note-taking, for remembering information and for organizing ideas for written work. The Inspiration program converts this image into a linear outline.

The latest version of Kidspiration (accessed January 2012) offers new capabilities including over 3,000 symbols, keyword symbol search, Word Guide, auditory support, visual maths tools, and additional curriculum materials. These help to give students opportunities to explore new learning concepts, discover meaning and express themselves with pictures, text, numbers and spoken words.

Ginger Software (www.gingersoftware.com)

The Ginger Software has been very well evaluated and is used a great deal in school. The grammar check in particular can be extremely helpful for the student with dyslexia. It includes preposition correction, verb correction, subject verb agreement, pronouns, singular/ plural nouns, misused words correction and contextually spelling correction. There is also a text-to-speech review.

Teacher modelling

Wray (2002) suggests that teacher modelling can be useful in developing reading and writing skills. He describes the background to shared reading and the metacognitive modelling approaches of Tonjes (1988) as a way for teachers to demonstrate to children the monitoring strategies they use in their own reading. He strongly advocates that teachers should model mental processes (what they think as they read or write) rather than simply procedures (what they do). Only in this way can children learn strategies that they can apply across a range of situations rather than merely being limited to the context in which they were encountered. Wray argues that the real benefits of shared reading result not just from teachers reading aloud to a group of learners, but from their thinking aloud at the same time.

   This approach and also shared writing are powerful teaching strategies and involve much more than just writing down what children say (like a competent secretary to their authors). Wray suggests that shared writing provides teachers opportunities to:

- Work with the whole class, to model, explore and discuss the decisions that writers make when they are writing.
- Make links between reading and writing explicit.
- Demonstrate how writers use language to achieve particular effects.
- Remove temporarily some of the problems of orchestrating writing skills by taking on the burden of some aspects, for example spelling and handwriting, thereby enabling the children to focus exclusively on how composition works.
- Focus on particular aspects of the writing process, such as planning, composing, revising or editing.
- 'Scaffold' children in the use of appropriate technical language to discuss what writers do and think.

This can be extremely beneficial for dyslexic children and can help to promote the metacognitive awareness that they sometimes find challenging. Additionally, it incorporates them more fully into the work of the whole class.

Self-questioning

It is important that children with dyslexia are encouraged and taught self-questioning. This will promote an enhanced awareness of the learning process. Wray (2002) describes a self-questioning procedure which consisted of the following questions, which children had to ask themselves as they read:

- First, I am going to decide if this story has any problems in it, like if one sentence says one thing and another sentence says something different or opposite.
- Second, as I read I will ask myself, 'Is there anything wrong with the story?'
- Third, I will read two sentences and stop and ask if anything is wrong.
- Fourth, so far, so good, I am doing a great job. Now I will read the whole story and decide if there are any problems in the whole story.
- Did I find any problems in this story?

Although children with dyslexia may have difficulty in reading fluently it is important that top-down and metacognitive approaches such as those described above are utilised. Essentially, one of the aims of education for children with dyslexia is the promotion of self-sufficiency in learning.

Other support approaches

Some other approaches that can be adapted from individualised programmes and used to support classroom work are briefly described below. These approaches can readily be adapted and utilised within curriculum frameworks.

Teaching Literacy to Learners with Dyslexia: a Multisensory Approach (Kelly and Philips 2011)

The book is a teaching manual and provides a structured programme for teaching literacy to children and young people with dyslexia and specific literacy difficulties. It also incorporates and links theory, research, and practice. The structured, cumulative, multi-sensory teaching programme also draws attention to learning styles and differences of learners with dyslexia such as memory, information processing, and automaticity. It also considers learners with English as an additional language (EAL). It is grounded in up-to-date research. The book provides a clear rationale and practical explanations of literacy concepts and conventions and therefore should simplify the task of dealing with the literacy challenges for many teachers.

Phonological awareness approaches

There is strong evidence to suggest that phonological factors are of considerable importance in reading (Rack, 1994; Wilson and Frederickson, 1995; Snowling, 2000). Children with decoding problems appear to be considerably hampered in reading because they are unable to generalise from one word to another. This means that every word they read is unique, indicating that there is a difficulty in learning and applying phonological rules in reading. This emphasises the importance of teaching sounds/ phonemes and ensuring that the child has an awareness of the sound/letter correspondence. Learning words by sight can enable some children to reach a certain standard in reading, but prevents them from adequately tackling new words and extending their vocabulary.

If children have a phonological awareness difficulty they are more likely to guess the word from the first letter cue and not the first **sound**, i.e. the word 'KITE' will be tackled from the starting point of the letter 'K' and not the sound 'ki', so the dyslexic reader may well read something like 'KEPT'. It is important, therefore, that beginner readers receive some structured training in the grapheme/phoneme correspondence; this is particularly necessary for dyslexic children who would not automatically, or readily, appreciate the importance of phonic rules in reading.

Paired reading

Paired reading as indicated earlier may be particularly useful for children with dyslexia since it provides both visual and auditory input simultaneously. It is a relatively straightforward technique that focuses on the following:

- Parent and child reading together.
- Programme to be carried out consistently.
- Child selects reading material.
- As few distractions as possible.
- Use of praise as reinforcement.
- Discussion of the story and pictures.

Toe by Toe: A Multi-sensory Manual for Teachers & Parents (Cowling and Cowling, 1993)

This is a multisensory teaching method highly recommended for teachers and parents. The programme has a multisensory element, a phonic element and some focus on the student's memory through the planning and the timing of each of the lessons in the book. It can be readily used by parents and the instructions are very clear. The same author has also published a programme called *Stride Ahead – An Aid to Comprehension* (Cowling, 2001), which can be a useful follow up to 'Toe by Toe'. Essentially 'Stride Ahead' has been written for children who can read but may have difficulty in understanding what they are reading.

Learning strategies

Reciprocal teaching and scaffolding

Reciprocal teaching and scaffolding are both viewed as metacognitive strategies and, therefore, aim to promote self-sufficiency in learning.

Green (2012) suggests that this concept is also vitally important for adult learners. Many she argues who have not succeeded at school lack confidence in their skills as a learner and are more likely to have a dependency on a tutor or teacher. Reciprocal teaching and scaffolding therefore need to be used with adults as well as younger children.

Reciprocal teaching refers to a procedure which both monitors and enhances comprehension by focusing on processes relating to questioning, clarifying, summarizing and predicting (Palincsar and Brown, 1984). This is an interactive process and one that can help enhance the thinking and problem-solving skills of children with dyslexia. Brown (1993) describes the procedure for reciprocal teaching as one that is initially led by the teacher. The teacher leads the discussion by asking questions and this generates additional questions from participants. The questions are then clarified by teacher and participants together. The discussion is summarised by the teacher or participants, and a new 'teacher' is selected by the participants to lead the discussion on the next section of the text.

'Scaffolding' describes the series of supports that can be built through teacher–pupil interaction to develop the understanding of text. This can be in the form of the teacher either providing the information or generating appropriate responses through questioning and clarifying. The supports are then withdrawn gradually, when the learner has achieved the necessary understanding to continue with less support.

Role-play to foster understanding

There is a great deal of evidence supporting the benefits of pre-reading discussion for the enhancement of both comprehension and decoding of text. Brozo (2003) develops this theme by suggesting that pre-reading strategies should involve active role-play techniques. He suggests that role-play strategies can help to accomplish reading readiness. Therefore, before introducing new learning to children, the teacher needs to consider how the story can be translated into relevant experiences for them. He suggests that the planning steps for role-play need careful attention and should include the teacher asking questions such as 'What are the human forces behind the events?', 'How can the story impact on people?' and 'How can the content be personalised for the class?' Role-play activities should also leave scope for pupils to utilise creativity so that the students can personalize the situation. This can help the pupils call to mind relevant prior knowledge, encourage student participation and provide the pupils with a purpose for exploring the new text and the new learning. This can be of considerable benefit for children with dyslexia as it can provide a framework for learning and help to clarify some of the key ideas of the new text.

Study skills

Study skills are essential for dyslexic children. There is some evidence that dyslexic children require particular help in this area, principally due to their organizational difficulties. A well-constructed study skills programme, therefore, is essential and can do much to enhance concept development, metacognitive awareness, transfer of learning and success in the classroom.

Such programmes will vary with the age and stage of the learner. A study skills programme for primary children would be different from that which may help students cope with examinations at secondary level. Well-developed study skills at the primary stage can provide a sound foundation for tackling new material in secondary school and help equip the student for examinations. Some of the principal factors in a study skills programme which will be discussed in this section include the following:

- Communication skills.
- Transfer of knowledge and skills.
- Mapping and visual skills.
- Memory skills.

In relation to study skills and memory training in particular the resources by Learning Works ® (**www.learning-works.org.uk**) are worth investigating. They have a wide range of well tried and successful resources for study skills.

Organization

Children with dyslexia may require help to organize their thoughts. A structure should therefore be developed to help encourage this. It may not be enough to ask children, for example on completion of a story, 'What was the story about?' They need to be provided with a structure in order to elicit correct responses. This helps with the organization of responses (output), which in turn can help to organize learning through comprehension (input). A structure which the teacher might use to elicit organized responses may include:

- What was the title?
- Who were the main characters?
- Describe the main characters.
- What did the main characters try to do?
- Who were the other characters in the story?
- What was the story about?
- What was the main part of the story?
- How did the story end?

In this way a structure is provided for the learner to retell the story. Moreover, the learner will be organizing the information into a number of components such as 'characters', 'story', 'conclusion'. This will not only make it easier for learners to retell orally, but will help to give them an organizational framework which will facilitate the retention of detail. The learner will also be using a strategy which can be used in other contexts. This will help with the new learning and the retention of new material.

Memory skills

Children with dyslexic difficulties may have difficulties in remembering, retaining and recalling information. This may be due to working memory and short-term memory problems (BPS, 1999a) or naming difficulty, particularly at speed, i.e. difficulty in recalling the name or description of something without cues (Wolf and O'Brien, 2001). It is important to encourage the use of strategies that may facilitate remembering and recall. Such strategies can include repetition and overlearning, the use of mnemonics and Mind Mapping©.

Repetition and overlearning

Short-term memory difficulties can be overcome by repetition and rehearsal of materials. This form of overlearning can be achieved in a variety of ways and not necessarily through conventional, and often tedious, rote learning.

In order to maximize the effect of repetition of learning it is important that a multisensory mode of learning is utilised. Repetition of the material to be learned can be accomplished through oral, visual, auditory and kinaesthetic modes. The learner should be able to say, see, hear and touch the materials to be learned. This reinforces the input stimuli and helps to consolidate the information for use, meaning and transfer to other areas. There are implications here for multi-mode teaching, including the use of movement, perhaps drama, to enhance the kinaesthetic mode of learning.

Mnemonics

Mnemonics can be auditory or visual, or both auditory and visual. Auditory mnemonics may take the form of rhyming or alliteration, while visual mnemonics can be used by relating the material to be remembered to a familiar scene, such as the classroom.

Mind Mapping©

Mind Mapping© was developed by Buzan to help children and adults develop their learning skills and utilize as much of their abilities as possible. The procedure is now widely used and can extend memory capacity and develop lateral thinking (Buzan, 1993). It can be a simple or a sophisticated strategy depending on how it is developed and used by the individual. It is used to help the learner to remember a considerable amount of information and encourages students to think of, and develop, the main ideas of a passage or material to be learned.

Essentially mind maps are individual learning tools and someone else's mind map may not be meaningful to you. It is important, therefore, that children should create their own, in order to help with both understanding of key concepts and in the retention and recall of associated facts.

Mind Mapping© can help not only in remembering information, but also in helping organize that information. This exercise in itself can aid understanding. Elaborate versions of mind maps can be constructed using pictorial images, symbols and different colours.

Planning for learning in the secondary school

Provision and practice

One of the key issues in relation to successful outcomes in secondary school concerns the notion of responsibility. It is important to ensure that the needs of dyslexic children are met and that all members of staff become fully involved.

The school management need to ensure that:

- The ethos of the school is supportive. The philosophy of the school together with attitudes and actions are known to all staff, including part-time support and other staff.
- All staff should be encouraged to acknowledge that with effective differentiation the curriculum can be accessed by dyslexic children.
- All teaching staff need to be supported in order to utilize some of the suggestions shown above in relation to planning, presentation and the development of materials.

● Parents need to be considered. They can offer very rich support in the form of information and assistance and it is important that collaboration between home and school is ongoing.

Accessing subject content

It can be suggested that if the subject materials and teaching plans are developed and implemented in a manner that is compatible with dyslexic students, students should be able to perform on the same terms as their peers. Although most of the subject content is determined by examination and prescribed curricular considerations, much can still be done to identify the potential areas of the curriculum that may present difficulties for dyslexic students.

There is no reason, therefore, why the content of all subjects cannot be developed in a dyslexia-friendly manner. It can be argued that the principles for making information dyslexia-friendly are the same for every subject. The key to achieving this is forward planning together with an awareness of dyslexia. This also implies an awareness of differentiation, learning styles and dyslexia-friendly assessment procedures.

Some examples of this are shown below for different subject areas of the curriculum.

English

In English it is important to use a range of sources, for example in literature, so that the dyslexic student can access a novel or play. It is often best to begin with discussion so that the overall story and plot can be understood before any reading begins. This also fits in with the learning style of many dyslexic students, as these appear to favour holistic processing as opposed to analytical. This means that the learner would need to understand the ideas and the background to the novel before reading it. This also helps to build concepts and schema. Schema essentially refers to the student's own understanding of a situation or an event. It is important that the student has an appropriate schema before commencing to read. Having a schema or framework will help the reader use context and understanding to help read difficult words, and indeed understand the novel without actually reading every word.

There are many aspects relating to English that can be challenging for students with dyslexia – expressive writing, spelling, grammar, as well as reading accuracy and fluency.

It is important to acknowledge the different types of reading activities and the different strategies that can be used for each. Reading examination questions and reading instructions will require a detailed and accurate form of reading. For the student with dyslexia this will mean that additional time will be necessary and they can produce a checklist to ensure they have understood the instructions. Such a list could include –What is actually being said/asked? What is required of me? How will I know if I am right? In other words the teacher is encouraging the student to think about the implications of the question/ instructions and to consider the information gleaned in different ways. By doing this it should become apparent to the student whether the question has been misread.

Similarly, in reading for facts the reader can make a checklist of different types of information under different headings. It may also be helpful if the teacher actually provides the headings for the student. The student with dyslexia needs to obtain practice in scanning and reading to obtain a general overview or impression of the text. One way to practice scanning is to give the learner a passage to read, but not give them sufficient time to read the passage. This means they will be forced to read only the key words.

These factors emphasise the importance of forward planning and breaking challenging areas down into smaller components. This means that the teacher will be able to identify which of these aspects present the most challenges and then work through the range of strategies that can be used for these areas. Some of the strategies include those that can be used for good teaching in general – teaching in a multisensory manner, helping to boost the student's memory through the use of mnemonics, personal spelling notebooks, the use of ICT to help with reading and the use of the Internet to investigate topics. It can sometimes be useful if the student with dyslexia can work in groups as he/ she can share skills with others in the group. The reading part can be done by someone else in the group while the dyslexic person can deal with some of the other aspects of the task.

Geography

Geography is a subject that can be accessed by dyslexic students. It has the potential to be highly visual and the subject content relates to the study of people and activities in the community and world around us. In other words it is a subject that has direct relevance to living in today's world. This means that information in geography can be accessed in a variety of ways – field trips, visually, visits, interviews and observation, quite apart from using reading materials.

In geography, as in many of the other subject areas, alternatives to the written answer can be used to a great extent. It is important that geography is underpinned by understanding and this is why active participatory learning is essential for dyslexic learners. It is crucial that the skills and abilities of dyslexic students in the areas of visual processing and understanding are not restricted because of lack of access to print materials. It was interesting to note that in the interviews conducted by Williams and Lewis (2001) with dyslexic students studying geography, one of the recurrent themes reported by the students was lack of opportunities to show their knowledge.

History

History is a subject that can be stimulating and engaging for the dyslexic student. It essentially demands investigation and skills in problem-solving, but too often the actual demands placed on the student relate to memory demands and the learning of massive amounts of facts. This of course need not be the case and it is necessary to consider ways in which the student might acquire the necessary information without resorting to rote memorization.

Dargie (2001) suggests that discussion holds the key to this. Talking about issues, he suggests, can help pupils rehearse the separate components of a topic and develop an argument that they can then use in written work.

At the same time the student with dyslexia can develop his/her own timeline. This can help the student memorize information within a sequence – an aspect that is challenging for students with dyslexia.

Contributing to a discussion exercise, or a group presentation, can have positive consequences for the dyslexic learner's self-esteem. Working in groups can also provide learners with practice at experimenting and becoming more familiar with their own learning style. It is important, according to Dargie, that students with dyslexia gain experience in the range of specific skills needed for history, such as the ability to question, infer, deduce, propose, estimate, guess, judge and to think.

Learning to talk about history can provide a launch pad for reading and writing about history. Similarly, paired homework, with an emphasis upon pupils having to check that their partner can readily explain topic vocabulary, can also provide the confidence to write. It is important to plan and anticipate the types of difficulties the student with dyslexia may experience in history. One example of this can be listening skills. Listening skills can be enhanced by providing dyslexic pupils with topic content in audio cassette form for individual use in iPod-type players. Many excellent audio resources exist for most history courses, particularly those broadcast by the BBC. Although there are difficulties in listening to audio programmes, the practice can be beneficial, and they can be valuable in helping individual learners rehearse topic vocabulary before a lesson, or for reinforcement purposes.

According to Dargie (2001, p. 76), it is also important that history departments plan a reading strategy that seeks to create 'more self-aware' readers who understand the purpose of their reading and who appreciate how and why the text in front of them is shaped in the way that it is. An effective reading strategy in history might include the following features:

- Consistent teacher pre-checking of text material and calculation of reading age to ensure pupils encounter historical text in a planned, progressive way.
- A focus upon concept vocabulary and upon discursive connectives which develop historical argument.
- The selective use of word processing functions such as emboldening and/or increasing font size to highlight the way historical text works.
- The planned reading of material as homework to increase pupil familiarity with the demands of the text using scissors and highlighter pens to analyse how different kinds of historical text are constructed.
- Highlighting photocopied text to given criteria (e.g. in search of key phrases).
- Persistent teacher questioning to accompany pupil reading to check comprehension. This is particularly important when working with dyslexic readers who may only have partially automatised the decoding of print, and who may not yet be self-generating questions as they read.
- Teacher awareness of the different preferred reading styles of pupils, and of the interactive nature of effective reading.
- Teacher awareness of the difficulties posed by 'weasel words' in history such as class, state, party and church, which have an abstract historical usage in addition to their more familiar common concrete meaning.
- Teacher alertness to the difficulties posed by subject-specific conventions such as 'c.' for 'circa', 'iv' for 'fourth', 'c.' for 'century', etc.
- Teacher awareness of the need to structure their own text to meet the needs of different learners, e.g. by avoiding long, multi-clausal sentences, avoiding over-use of passive voice constructions, planning ways of explaining unfamiliar vocabulary and ideas, e.g. word boxes and marginal scaffolding, keeping text concrete where appropriate rather than abstract, minimizing the use of metaphorical language, and being alert to the range of tenses used in history to describe actions in the past.

Examinations can cause considerable anxiety for students with dyslexia and this can be dealt with by the history department through recognition of the kind of exam anxiety dyslexic students can experience. It is also useful to provide specific study skills aimed at examination revision and ensuring that the student revises effectively and uses the time available efficiently. It is often the case that students with dyslexia spend a considerable length of time revising, but often to no avail – it is important then that such student effort is rewarded. Guidance and support in study and study techniques, therefore, is as crucial as the students' knowledge and understanding of the actual content of the subject.

Physics

Physics is a subject that can present some difficulties to dyslexic students, but it is also one of the subjects in which they can do well because it may involve less reading and a high degree of scientific understanding. Holmes (2001) suggests a top-down approach, first providing a whole-school awareness of dyslexia and allowing subject teachers to reflect on the implications of providing for dyslexic students in their own subject. Other factors which Holmes considers include:

- Building a bank of support materials that can become a whole-school resource.
- Recognizing the implications of secondary difficulties which can affect a student's performance in a particular subject – e.g. the relationship between mathematics and physics, which can mean that the student's difficulties in physics are a consequence of Mathematics difficulties.

These emphasize the need for a whole-school approach on dealing with dyslexia.

Drama

Drama is also a subject that should be enjoyable and easily accessed by students with dyslexia – often, however, it is not. There is much more to drama than reading plays and it is important that the dyslexic person becomes actively involved in all aspects of drama.

This can include planning the sets and designing costumes. Gray (2001) suggests that students can perhaps work in pairs through the various scenes in a play, complete columns with lists of props, character costumes, and ideas for scenery. Eadon (2002) suggests that many ideas can come from the students themselves and it is important to allow students to take some initiative, especially since students with dyslexia can have some very innovative ideas. This of course can also help to boost self-esteem.

One of the important aspects about drama is that it has cross-curricular implications. Drama can have a positive spin-off effect in English, art and other subjects. Subjects such as drama have the opportunity to boost a student's self-concept and this can have a transferable effect to other subject areas.

Implications for other subjects

The examples above highlight how different subject areas can be accessed for dyslexic children. They also illustrate that the suggestions, and the principles upon which these suggestions are based, can be applied across the whole curriculum. All subjects, including the sciences and the social sciences and subjects of a more practical and technical orientation, can be made dyslexia-friendly. The key principles include planning as well as an awareness of dyslexia and the difficulties and strengths shown by students with dyslexia. It is also important to recognize the role of learning styles and the need to present information in a manner and mode that is consistent with the learner's learning style. One cannot underestimate the potential of cross-curricular learning and the importance of this for students with dyslexia. Of great importance is the development of self-esteem – this usually comes from success and it is crucial that the student with dyslexia experiences success in at least some of the subject areas. But all subject teachers can make accommodations to meet the needs of dyslexic students and clearly planning and differentiation are essential to achieve this.

Key issues

Some of the key issues relating to dyslexia in the secondary school include:

- The subject content – ensuring it is accessible.
- Subject delivery – ensuring that the presentation of the curriculum acknowledges the learning style and the strengths of students with dyslexia and that the planning takes into account the potential difficulties they may experience with the subject.
- Assessment – as far as possible a wide range of assessment strategies should be used.
- Cross-curricular aspects – it is important that opportunities for collaboration with other subject teachers are provided as this can promote any cross-curricular transfer of knowledge and enables any particular concepts that can apply across different subject areas to be noted.
- Learning styles – it is important to acknowledge the fact that new learning needs to be presented in a manner that can suit the student's learning style.
- Training for staff in the area of dyslexia is important as all staff should have at least an awareness of dyslexia.

It is important that these issues are fully addressed in order that the student with dyslexic difficulties can achieve some success in different subject areas. Teaching and learning should be planned together. This implies that knowledge of teaching strategies and the learner's individual strengths, difficulties and learning style are necessary in order for planning and presentation of learning to be effective.

Other subjects such as modern foreign languages, art and design, and design and technology, which can prove challenging in terms of the amount of reading, can lend themselves quite easily to kinaesthetic approaches by focusing on experiential learning activities.

For example, modern languages is often seen as a source of considerable difficulty for the dyslexic student and consequently frustration for the teacher. Crombie and McColl (2001) show that by using appropriate strategies and considering the mode of presentation, dyslexic students can achieve success.

For example they suggest the following:

- The use charts and diagrams to highlight the bigger picture.
- Adding mime and gesture to words.
- Adding pictures to text.
- Using colour to highlight gender or accents.
- Labelling diagrams and charts.
- Using games to consolidate vocabulary.

- Making packs of pocket-sized cards.
- Using different colours for different purposes.
- Combining listening and reading by providing text and tape.
- Using mind maps, spidergrams.
- Allowing students to produce their own audio tapes.
- Presenting information in small chunks, using a variety of means, with frequent opportunities for repetition and revision.
- Providing an interest in the country, through showing films, and highlighting literature and culture.

Generally it is important in most subjects for instructions to be short and clear, preferably using bullet points. It is also worth considering the use of labels and key terms to highlight various points – the dyslexic student often has a word-finding difficulty and may need some of the terms used in some subject areas to be reinforced.

Comment

The points made in this chapter and in the previous two chapters highlight the view that supporting students with dyslexia is a whole-school responsibility. This view is supported by the work of prominent authors – Barbara Pavey in her book *The Dyslexia-Friendly Primary School* (Pavey 2007), Tilly Mortimore and Jane Dupree in *Dyslexia Friendly Practice in the Secondary School* (Mortimore and Dupree 2008) and Neil Mackay in *Removing Dyslexia as a Barrier to Achievement* (Mackay 2008). These views all consistently advocate whole-school awareness of dyslexia and strategies and approaches that can maintain the learners' self-esteem and can ensure access to the full mainstream curriculum. Pavey sums this up when she remarks that most of the ideas are 'practitioner's craft knowledge': '... it is important that practitioners believe they can make a difference when children experience dyslexia and to appreciate that they have craft knowledge to call upon for this purpose' (Pavey 2007, pp. 1–2).

7 Concluding comments

Flexibility

This book has maintained the position that a flexible approach is required when dealing with dyslexia in the classroom. There is no 'off-the-shelf' answer to dyslexia. There are many key factors that play a role in supporting students with dyslexia.

1. The curriculum.
2. The task.
3. The level and scope for implementing differentiation.
4. Knowledge of the student's individual learning style.
5. The availability of a comprehensive and contextualized assessment at the outset of intervention.
6. The presence of co-ordinated planning.
7. A recognition by school management of the needs of teachers in supporting students with dyslexia.
8. Opportunities for appropriate and practical training for the whole school staff.

If these factors are acknowledged then all students with dyslexia can be included in the mainstream, or at least have full access to the mainstream curriculum.

The term 'inclusion' implies that the needs of all children should be met within the mainstream school. But in order for children with difficulties such as dyslexia to have their needs fully met in mainstream school there is a need for all teachers to be at least familiar with a range of intervention approaches and resources for dyslexia. It is suggested here that the responsibility for meeting the needs of children with dyslexia should not necessarily rest in the hands of specialists. Certainly those teachers who have specialist training and experience play a vitally important role. They can pass on their skills to class teachers and help to ensure that all staff have an awareness and some training in the different aspects of dyslexia. Additionally some children with dyslexia will also need specialist 'top-up' intervention such as those approaches indicated in Chapter 6 and developed by organizations such as Dyslexia Action and the Helen Arkell Dyslexia Centre in the UK and the Orton Gillingham Approach in the USA and Canada.

In order for inclusion to be achieved at the school level, co-ordinated curriculum planning and shared objectives between home and school are required and the development of individual programmes of work can help to achieve this. Consultation and planning are two of the key factors that can bring about inclusion and full access to the curriculum.

This book advocates that dyslexia should not be viewed from a narrow perspective, but from one that is multi-faceted. For that reason it is important that teachers have a full understanding of the different dimensions that can contribute to dyslexia. The view discussed in Chapter 1 of dyslexia as a difference is a helpful one and can assist teachers to recognize the needs of children with dyslexia and particularly the need to look beyond the label.

It is for this reason that two of the chapters (Chapters 5 and 6) are devoted to supporting the learner to develop more effective learning strategies. Those chapters also discuss a range of strategies that can help to develop cognitive and thinking skills. These include the need to develop memory skills, to make connections between existing knowledge and new information, and to generally acknowledge the information-processing style and difficulties experienced by children with dyslexia. While it is appreciated that dyslexic children share common difficulties and processing styles, the individual differences also need to be recognized.

The challenge is to acknowledge these differences while dealing with the everyday demands of classroom teaching. One way of doing this is through recognition of learning styles. Learning styles can help to equip the child with self-knowledge and this can in turn lead to autonomy in learning. This is vital for children with dyslexia, as they will not always have a support teacher, or a class teacher, to assist their learning.

The other challenge is the central one of responding to the needs of children with dyslexia within a mainstream setting and within the demands of the school curriculum. This can be achieved partly through effective differentiation, but above all, by forward planning. Planning for learning and identifying and anticipating the aspects of the curriculum that will be difficult for dyslexic children are vital.

Many of these challenges are discussed in Chapter 2 of this book. It is worth noting Baroness Warnock's comments (Chapter 2) 'including all children in the common educational enterprise of learning, wherever they learn best' (Warnock, 2005: p. 14). The key is not where or how, it is not an equality issue, it is a learning issue. The key is the impact the learning has on the student. If it is not working, then there must be mechanisms for change. Although there needs to be a key role for classroom teachers in supporting students with dyslexia, it is also important to recognize the expertise and experience that specialist practitioners have built up over the years (Bell and McLean 2012). Norwich's (2009) reference to a flexible interacting continua of provision has considerable merit when one considers the range of characteristics evident in dyslexia and the other co-existing and associated difficulties. Within these challenges and responses it is also crucially important to recognize the wishes and needs of parents. Any intervention programme will be considerably more effective if there is parental collaboration. It has been stated in Chapter 2 that communication is the key in dealing with any potential conflicts that may occur between home and school.

The idea of a dyslexia toolkit is highlighted in Chapter 3. Such a toolkit includes identification as well as intervention strategies. Initiatives in the UK such as Say No to Failure (www. xtraordinarypeople.com) and the popular and influential Inclusion Index (revised and updated; Booth *et al.*, 2011) as well as initiatives in the USA such as the Individuals with Disabilities Education Act (IDEA; US Government 2001) and the Response to Intervention (RTI) model can all steer a path to supporting mainstream teachers in dealing with the classroom challenges presented by students with dyslexia and other similar difficulties.

There are three key aspects of support: planning of learning, presentation of lessons, and differentiation and accessibility of materials. There is a tendency to focus on the materials, suggesting that with the right resources and materials dyslexic children will be able to learn effectively. Appropriate resources are vital but this does not preclude the need for the teacher to embark on curricular planning and differentiation as a means of meeting the needs of dyslexic children. It is perhaps more helpful to view the difficulties experienced by dyslexic children as barriers to learning. It follows that if these barriers can be identified through examining the curriculum and the tasks presented to the child, then this will go a long way towards meeting these needs.

The need for training

As indicated earlier, there is no 'off-the-shelf' ready-made answer or programme that suits all dyslexic children. It is necessary for the teacher to be flexible and versatile in the development of resources and teaching strategies. For that reason it is indicated in this book that training for class teachers in the area of dyslexia is crucial. This training does not need to be highly specialised, but should include an awareness of the difficulties associated with dyslexia, how these can be identified and how they can be overcome within the curriculum. By taking a curriculum perspective one can more readily identify the barriers to learning and the tasks and the aspects of the curriculum that the child with dyslexia may have difficulties with. This is highlighted particularly in Chapter 4 on curriculum access. All teachers need to be aware of the barriers to learning that can be experienced by children and young people with dyslexia as well as the different stages of the assessment process, particularly observation. It is crucial that all class teachers through observation and interacting with the student are able to pick up the early warning signs of dyslexia. The assessment framework developed through Dyslexia Scotland and the Scottish Government by Crombie and colleagues (www.frameworkforinclusion.org/ AssessingDyslexia, accessed October 2011) provides an excellent example of how this can be achieved in practice.

Training courses should also include quick tips for teachers that can help them support students with dyslexia in the classroom – at both primary and secondary stages (and also in tertiary education). The information developed by Thomson (2008) and highlighted in Chapter 4 is a significant boost to the bank of support resources available for subject teachers in secondary school. The issue of supporting secondary teachers is developed further in Chapter 6 on practical approaches by referring to a number of different subjects in the secondary curriculum. The significance of the Rose Review on Dyslexia (2009) in the UK is also referred to in that chapter.

There are of course some well-founded principles for teaching children with dyslexia. These include multisensory teaching and learning and overlearning to develop automaticity. Multisensory approaches are important because children with dyslexia can have difficulty in learning through the auditory modality and therefore need visual, kinaesthetic and tactile stimuli in order for information to be processed. Overlearning is necessary in order to achieve automaticity so that learning can be consolidated. It has been shown that dyslexic children often take longer to develop automaticity and if they do not use a skill or word regularly they may forget it (see Fawcett and Reid, 2009).

Regular practice in reading and using words in a multisensory manner in different contexts is crucial. It is also crucial that children with dyslexia gain experience in the use of language. This means that top-down approaches to reading focusing on language experience are necessary even though the child may still not have basic word attack skills. Learning to read involves a mixture of both bottom-up phonic skills and top-down language experiences. Both can help to build decoding skills and the development of concepts and ideas. Both are essential aspects of reading. There is a tendency to neglect the development of concepts and higher-order thinking skills with dyslexic children because of their difficulties in decoding. But decoding should not take priority over the development of higher-order thinking skills. Reading is not only about accessing print, but about understanding the meaning of text and transmitting cultural and conceptual understanding to the reader. This should encourage metacognitive thinking and questioning, which in turn can develop self-sufficiency in learning.

One of the aims of this book is to dispel any myths and misconceptions about dyslexia such as those often seen in media reports of 'miracle cures' and 'new breakthroughs'. What is needed is not a miracle cure but for teachers to gain a full understanding of dyslexia that will help them evaluate the merits of innovative or alternative approaches and how to use the established approaches more effectively.

It is too easy to be swayed by vigorous marketing and commercial activities.

This book and particularly Chapters 5 and 6 have indicated that differentiation, awareness of learning styles and the learning environment, and a full understanding of dyslexia can go a long way to supporting and ensuring that the learning potential of dyslexic children is maximized, within the mainstream setting.

Inclusion is currently a key theme in education and this presents considerable challenges to teachers, particularly those with some responsibility for children with specific difficulties such as dyslexia. But it is important to recognize that each child offers an individual set of challenges to teachers and schools. It is for that reason that Chapter 6 contains details of the importance of Individual Education Plans (IEPs) and Personal Learning Plans (PLPs). Individual Education Plans (IEPs) can provide a means of ensuring the needs of children are met within the educational setting.

Self-esteem

One of the key aspects is the acknowledgement of self-esteem and every effort should be made, irrespective of the setting, to boost the self-esteem of children with dyslexia. This can be achieved through success and it is crucial that attainable goals are set in order that success can be achieved in some form. An understanding of dyslexia and knowledge of the child's learning preferences are necessary to help achieve this.

Collaboration

One cannot underestimate the challenge faced by teachers of ensuring that the needs of dyslexic children are met in the mainstream school. It is possible to deal with this by ensuring that the school management, parents and all staff involved with the student meet and have a constructive and respectful relationship. Education policy is important and there are already many excellent examples of sound and innovative policy on dyslexia paying dividends in practice, such as the dyslexia-friendly schools campaign in the UK which has done a great deal to ensure that dyslexia is not seen as a within-child deficit, but as the responsibility of the school and one that needs to be shared by all. This is consistent with the theme of this book and it is hoped that teachers and management will appreciate the need for training and collaboration, in order to provide all staff with an awareness of the needs of dyslexic children, together with the implications of this for curriculum development, the classroom environment and educational policy. Inclusion is more than an ideal, it is a process that every school needs to be engaged in and every child has the right to experience. With understanding, informative training, resources and commitment this ideal can become a reality.

Further information and contacts

Website – **www.drgavinreid.com** (contains links to most of the relevant organizations in literacy and dyslexia, including government organizations).

The Dyslexia Handbook; BDA, 98 London Road, Reading, RG1 5AU (published annually).

Materials from Dyslexia Action – e.g., Active Literacy Kit and Units of Sound (see www.dyslexiaaction.org.uk/Pages/Category.aspx?CategoryTitle=dasl&IDCategory= a890323d-989a-46f6-a035-eab310338aa5, accessed 29 December 2011).

Gavin Reid (2009), *Dyslexia – A Practitioners Handbook* (4th edn), Wiley.

Dyslexia: A complete guide for parents and those who help them (2nd edn) (2011) Gavin Reid, Wiley.

Dyslexia, An International Journal of Research and Practice; Fawcett, A. (ed.), Wiley.

Teaching the Literacy Hour in an Inclusive Classroom Supporting Pupils with Learning Difficulties in a Mainstream Environment; Ann Berger and Jean Gross (eds) (1999), David Fulton Publishers, London.

Get Ahead – Mind Map© Your Way to Success; Vanda North with Tony Buzan (2001), Buzan Centres, Worldwide.

Working towards Inclusive Education – Social Contexts; Peter Mittler (2000), David Fulton Publishers.

Special Educational Needs, Inclusion and Diversity, a textbook; Norah Frederickson and Tony Cline (2002), Open University Press, Buckingham, England.

Crossbow Education, 41 Sawpit Lane, Brocton, Stafford, ST17 0TE, www. crossboweducation.com.

Dyslexia: assessing the need for access arrangements (4th edn 2011), PATOSS edited by Anwen Jones.

Removing Dyslexia as a Barrier to Achievement, Neil Mackay (2008), Special Educational Needs Bookshop, www.senbooks.co.uk/view-product/Removing-Dyslexia-as-a-Barrier-to-Achievement.

The Trouble with Maths, 2nd edn (2010), Steve Chinn, David Fulton Books.

100 + Ideas for Supporting Students with Dyslexia, 2nd edn, Gavin Reid and Shannon Green (2011) Continuum Publications, London.

Pavey, B. (2007), *The Dyslexia-Friendly Primary School*: *A practical guide for teachers*, Sage Publications, UK.

Mortimore, T. and Dupree, J. (2008), *Dyslexia Friendly Practice in the Secondary School*, Learning Matters Ltd, Exeter, UK.

In L. Peer and G. Reid (eds.) 2012 *Special Educational Needs: A Guide for Inclusive Practice*, Sage Publications, London.

iANSYT Ltd, The White House, 72 Fen Road, Cambridge, CB4 1UN.

SEN Marketing Dyslexia and Special Needs Bookshop, www.senbooks.co.uk.

Contacts

British Dyslexia Association, 98 London Road, Reading,	www.bda-dyslexia.org.uk
DysGuise Ltd	www.dysguise.com
Learning Works International Ltd, 9 Barrow Close, Marlborough, Wiltshire SN8 2BD, UK.	www.learning-works.org.uk

Dyslexia Scotland	www.dyslexiascotland.org.uk
Northern Ireland Dyslexia Association	www.nida.org.uk
Dyslexia Association of Ireland	www.dyslexia.ie
Dyslexia Action	www.dyslexiaaction.org.uk
Helen Arkell Dyslexia Centre	www.arkellcentre.org.uk
Nottingham Dyslexia Association	www.dyslexia.uk.net
Dyslexic Advantage	http://dyslexicadvantage.com
Lighthouse School in Cairo	www.lighthouseschoolonline.com
	www.frameworkforinclusion.org.
	www.xtraordinarypeople.com
Red Rose School	www.redroseschool.co.uk
Global Educational Consultants	www.globaleducationalconsultants.com/
	projects.html
International Dyslexia Association	www.interdys.org
Professional Association of Teachers of Students with SpLDs	www.patoss-dyslexia.org
The Landmark School	www.landmarkschool.org
The Caroll School	www.carrollschool.org
The White Oak School	www.whiteoakschool.org
The Academy for Inclusion of Special Needs	www.globaleducationalconsultants.com/uk

www.frameworkforinclusion.org
www.xtraordinarypeople.com

References and further reading

Assessment Reform Group (1999) *Assessment for Learning: beyond the black box*, Cambridge: University of Cambridge School of Education.

Avramidis, E. and Norwich, B. (2012) SEN: The State of Research – compromise, consensus or disarray?, in L. Peer and G. Reid (eds), 2012, Special Educational Needs: A guide for inclusive practice, London, Sage Publications.

Bell, S. and McLean, B. (2012) Good Practice in Training Specialist Teachers and Assessors of People with Dyslexia in L. Peer and G. Reid (eds), *Special Educational Needs: A guide for inclusive practice*, London, Sage Publications.

Bond, J., Coltheart, M., Connell, T., Firth, N., Hardy, M., Nayton, M., *et al.* (2010) *Helping People with Dyslexia: A National Action Agenda*, Canberra.

Booth, T., Ainscow, M., Black-Hawkins, K., Vaughn, M. and Shaw, L. (2000) (revised 2011) *Index for Inclusion: Developing Learning and Participation in Schools*. Bristol: Centre for Studies in Inclusive Education (CSIE).

Breznitz, Z., (2008) The Origin of Dyslexia: The Asynchrony Phenomenon, in G. Reid, A. Fawcett, F. Manis and L. Siegel (eds), *The Sage Dyslexia Handbook*. London, Sage Publications.

British Dyslexia Association (BDA) (2011) The Dyslexia Handbook, Published annually. British Dyslexia Association (BDA)

British Psychological Society (BPS) (1999a) *Dyslexia, Literacy and Psychological Assessment.* Leicester: British Psychological Society.

British Psychological Society (1999b) *The Directory of Chartered Psychologists*. Leicester, BPS.

Brodhead, M. R. and Price, G., (1993) The Learning Styles of Artistically Talented Adolescents in Canada, in R. Milgram, R. Dunn, G. Price, (eds), *Teaching and Counselling Talented Adolescents: An International Perspective*, Praeger Westport. CT.

Bronfenbrenner, U. (1979), *The Ecology of Human Development*, Cambridge, MA, Harvard University Press.

Brown, A., Armbruster, B. and Baker, L. (1986) The Role of Metacognition in Reading and Studying, in Oraspinu, J. (ed.), *Reading Comprehension from Research to Practice*, Hillsdale, NJ, Lawrence Erlbaum.

Brown, A. L. and Campione, J. C. (1994) Guided Discovery in a Community of Learners, pp. 229–70 in K. McGilly (ed.), *Classroom Lessons: Integrating Cognitive Theory and Classroom Practice*. Cambridge, MA: MIT Press.

Brown, M. (1993) 'Supporting Learning Through a Whole-School Approach', in Reid, G (ed.), *Specific Learning Difficulties (Dyslexia) Perspectives on Practice.* Edinburgh, Moray House Publications.

Brozo, W. (2003) *Strategic Moves – role playing in thinking*, *an international journal of reading, writing and critical reflection,* vol. 4, No. 2 (April), pp. 43–5

Burden, B. (2002) 'A cognitive approach to dyslexia: Learning styles and thinking skills', in G. Reid and J. Wearmouth (eds), *Dyslexia and Literacy: Theory and Practice*. Wiley.

Buzan, T. (1993) *The Mind Map Book – Radiant Thinking* London, BBC Books.

Buzan, T. (2003) *Mind Maps for Kids*, Buzan Centre, UK.

Calder, I. (2001) 'Dyslexia across the Curriculum', in L. Peer and G. Reid (eds), *Dyslexia – Successful Inclusion in the Secondary School*. London, David Fulton Publishers.

Came, F. and Reid, G. (2008) *Concern, Assess Provide (CAP It All)*, Wiltshire, UK, Learning Works.

Clay, M. (1979) *Reading: The patterning of complex behaviour*. Auckland, Heinemann Educational.

Clay, M. (1985) *The Early Detection of Reading Difficulties: a diagnostic survey with recovery procedures*, Auckland, Heinemann Educational.

Coffield, F., Moseley, D., Hall, E. and Ecclestone, K. (2004) *Should We be Using Learning Styles? What research has to say to practice*, London, DfES.

Coffield, M., Riddick, B., Barmby, P and O'Neill, J. (2008) 'Dyslexia Friendly Primary Schools: what can we learn from asking the pupils?', in G. Reid, A. Fawcett, F. Manis and L. Siegel (eds) *The Sage Handbook of Dyslexia*, London, Sage Publications.

Conner, M. (1994) *Specific learning difficulties (dyslexia) and interventions*, Support for Learning, 9 (3) pp. 114–19.

Cooper, R. (2009) 'Dyslexia', in Pollak, D. (ed.) *Neurodiversity in Higher Education: Positive Responses to Specific Learning Differences*, Chichester, UK, Wiley, Blackwell.

Cowling, H. and Cowling, K. (1993) *Toe by Toe: Multi-sensory Manual for Teachers & Parents*, UK, Bradford.

Cowling, K. (2001) Stride Ahead: An aid to comprehension, Keda Publications, UK.

Crombie, M. (2002) 'Dealing with Diversity in the Primary Classroom: a challenge for the class teacher', in G. Reid and J. Wearmouth (eds) *Dyslexia and Literacy: theory and practice*, Wiley.

Crombie, M. and McColl, H. (2001) 'Dyslexia and the Teaching of Modern Foreign Languages', in L. Peer and G. Reid (eds), *Dyslexia – Successful Inclusion in the Secondary School*, London, David Fulton Publishers.

Crombie, M., Knight, D. and Reid, G. (2004) 'Dyslexia – Early Identification and Early Intervention: Perspectives from both sides of the Atlantic', in G. Reid and A. Fawcett (eds), *Dsylexia in Context: Research and practice*, pp. 1–24. London, Whurr Publications.

Crombie, M. and Reid, G. (2009) 'The Role of Early Identification: models from research and practice' in G. Reid (ed.), *The Routledge Companion to Dyslexia*, London, Routledge.

Cudd, E. T. and Roberts, L. L. (1994) 'A Scaffolding Technique to Develop Sentence Sense and Vocabulary', *The Reading Teacher*, 47(4), pp. 346–9.

Dargie, R. (2001) Dyslexia and History, in Peer, L. and G. Reid (eds), *Dyslexia: Successful Inclusion in the Secondary School*. London, David Fulton Publishers.

DES (1978) *Special Educational Needs* (The Warnock Report), London, HMSO.

Department for Education and Employment (DfEE) (1994) *The Code of Practice for the Identification and Assessment of Special Educational Needs*, London, DfEE.

Department for Education and Employment (DfEE) (1996) *The National Literacy Project*.

Department for Education and Employment (DfEE) (1998) *Framework for Teaching*.

Department for Education and Skills (2001) *Special Educational Needs Code of Practice*, London, DfEE.

DfEE and QCA (1999) *The National Curriculum for England: Geography*, London, DfEE and QCA.

DfES (2001) *Special Education Needs Code of Practice*, London, Department for Education and Skills.

Dimitriadi, Y. (2000) 'Using ICT to Support Bilingual Dyslexic Learners', in L. Peer and G. Reid (eds), *Multilingualism, Literacy and Dyslexia: A Challenge for Educators*, London, David Fulton Publishers.

Ditchfield, D. (2001) Dyslexia and Music, in L. Peer and G. Reid (eds), *Dyslexia: Successful Inclusion in the Secondary School*, London, David Fulton.

Dockrell, J. and McShane, J. (1993) Children's Learning Difficulties: A Cognitive Approach, Oxford, Blackwell.

Dodds, D. (1996) Differentiation in the Secondary School, in: G. Reid (ed.), *Dimensions of Dyslexia, vol. 1: Assessment, Teaching and the Curriculum*, Edinburgh, Moray House Publications.

Dunn, R. and Griggs, S. A. (1988) *Learning Styles: The Quiet Revolution in American Secondary Schools*, Reston, VA, USA, NASSP.

Dyslexia Scotland (2011) *Supporting Pupils with Dyslexia in the Primary* www.dyslexiascotland.org.uk

Eadon, H. (2002) *Dyslexia and Drama*, London, David Fulton Publishers.

Everatt, J. (2002) 'Visual Processes', in G. Reid and J. Wearmouth (eds), *Dyslexia and Literacy: Theory and Practice*, Wiley.

Everatt, J. and Reid, G. (2009). Dyslexia: An overview of recent research, In G. Reid (ed.), *The Routledge Companion to Dyslexia*, pp. 32–56. New York, NY: Routledge.

Farrell, P. (2001) Special Education in the Last Twenty Years: have things really got better?, *British Journal of Special Education* 28, pp. 3–9.

Fawcett, A. and Reid, G. (2009) 'Dyslexia and alternative interventions', in G. Reid (ed.), *The Routledge Companion to Dyslexia*, pp. 193–202, New York, NY: Routledge.

Fawcett, A. J. and Nicolson, R. I. (1996) *The Dyslexia Screening Test*, London, Psychological Corporation, Europe.

Fawcett, A. J. and Nicolson, R. I., (2001) 'Dyslexia: The Role of the Cerebellum', in A. J. Fawcett (ed.), *Dyslexia: Theory and Good Practice*. London, Whurr Publications.

Fawcett, A. and Nicolson, R. (2008) 'Dyslexia and the Cerebellum', in G. Reid, A. Fawcett, F. Manis and L. Siegel (2008) *The Sage Handbook of Dyslexia*, London, Sage Publications.

Fawcett, A., Nicolson, R. and Lee, R. (2001) *The Pre-school Screening Test (PREST)*, Kent, Psychological Corporation.

Flavell, J. H. (1979) 'Metacognition and cognitive monitoring', *American Psychologist*, October, pp. 906–11.

Florian, L. (2005) 'Inclusion', 'Special Needs' and the Search for New Understandings, *Support for Learning*, vol. 20, no.2, pp. 96–8.

Frith, U (2002) 'Resolving the Paradoxes of Dyslexia', in G. Reid and J. Wearmouth (eds), *Dyslexia and Literacy: Theory and Practice*. Wiley.

Galaburda, A. (ed.) (1993) *Dyslexia and Development: Neurobiological Aspects of Extraordinary Brains.* Cambridge, MA, Harvard University Press.

Gardner, H. (1983) *Frames of Mind*, New York, Basic Books.

Gardner, H. (1999) Foreword in D. Lazear *Eight Ways of Knowing Teaching for Multiple Intelligences*, 3rd edn, Skylight Professional Development, Arlington Heights, IL, USA, pp. vii–viii,

Garner, P. and Sandow, S. (1995) *Advocacy, Self-advocacy and Special Needs*, London, David Fulton.

Giorcelli, L. R. (1999) Inclusion and Other Factors Affecting Teachers Attitudes to Literacy Programs for Students with Special Needs, in A. J. Watson and L. R. Giorcelli (eds), *Accepting the Literacy Challenge*, Gosford, Australia, Scholastic.

Glyn, T. and McNaughton, S. (1985), The 'Managere' Home and School Remedial Reading Procedures: continuing research on their effectiveness, *New Zealand Journal of Psychology*, pp. 66–77.

Goodman, K. (1976) 'Reading: a psycholinguistic guessing game', in H. Singer and R. B. Ruddell, (eds), *Theoretical Models and Processes of Reading*, International Reading Association.

Gorrie, B. and Parkinson, E. (1995) *Phonological Awareness Procedure*, Stass Publications.

Government of Ireland (2001) Republic of Ireland was the Report of the Task Force on Dyslexia (July 2001).

Gray, R. (2001) 'Drama: The Experience of Learning', in L. Peer and G. Reid (eds), *Dyslexia – Successful Inclusion in the Secondary School*, London, David Fulton Publishers.

Green, S. (2012) Ideas into Action: Multisensory Structured Language Teaching. Workshop conducted at supporting Learners and Learning Differences: DTES PD Workshop Series April 13, 2012 Carnegie Learning Centre, Vancouver, BC, Canada.

Holmes, P. (2001) 'Dyslexia and Physics', in L. Peer and G. Reid (eds), *Dyslexia – Successful Inclusion in the Secondary School*, London, David Fulton Publishers.

Houston, M. (2011) *Supporting Pupils with Dyslexia at Primary School*, Stirling, Scotland, Dyslexia Scotland.

Hunt, G. (2002) 'Critical Literacy and Access to the Lexicon', in G. Reid and J. Wearmouth (eds), *Dyslexia and Literacy: theory and practice*, Wiley.

Hunter, V. (2001) 'Dyslexia and General Science', in L. Peer and G. Reid (eds) *Dyslexia – Successful Inclusion in the Secondary School*, London, David Fulton Publishers.

Irlen, H. L. (1991) *Reading by the Colors: Overcoming Dyslexia and other Reading Disabilities through the Irlen Method*, New York, Avebury Publishing.

Johnson, M. (2001) 'Inclusion: The Challenges' in L. Peer and G. Reid (eds), *Dyslexia – Successful Inclusion in the Secondary School*, London, David Fulton Publishers.

Johnson, M. and Peer, L. (eds) (2003) *The Dyslexia Handbook 2003*, Reading, BDA.

Johnson, M., Philips, S. and Peer, L. (1999) *Multisensory Teaching System for Reading*, Special Educational Needs Centre, Didsbury School of Education, Manchester Metropolitan University.

Kelly. K. and Philips, S. (2011) *Teaching Literacy to Learners with Dyslexia*, London, Sage Publications.

Kirk, J. (2001) 'Cross-Curricular Approaches to Staff Development in Secondary Schools', in L. Peer and G. Reid (eds), *Dyslexia – Successful Inclusion in the Secondary School*, London, David Fulton Publishers.

Landon, J. (1999) 'Early Intervention with Bilingual Learners: towards a research agenda', in H. South (ed.), *Literacies in Community and School,* Watford: National Association for Language Development in the Curriculum (NALDIC), pp. 84–96.

Lannen, S. and Reid, G. (2003) 'Learning Styles: Lights, Sound, Action', in *BDA Handbook 2003*, Reading, BDA.

Lazear, D. (1999) *Eight Ways of Knowing Teaching for Multiple Intelligences* 3rd edn, Skylight Professional Development, Arlington Heights, IL, USA.

Lindsay, G. (2003) Inclusive Education: a critical perspective. *British Journal of Special Education* 30 (1), 3–11.

Macintyre, C. and Deponio, P. (2003) *Identifying and supporting children with specific learning difficulties, looking beyond the label to assess the whole child*, Routledge/Falmer.

Mackay, N. (2008) *Removing Dyslexia as a Barrier to Achievement*, Wakefield, UK, SEN Books, http://senbooks.co.uk.

McLaughlin, M. and Allen, M. B. (2002) *Guided Comprehension: A teaching model for grades 3–8*, Newark, DE: International Reading Association.

McLean, A. (2008), *The Motivated School*, London, Sage Publications.

McLoughlin, D. and Leather, C. (2009), Dyslexia: Meeting the needs of employers and employees in the workplace, in G. Reid (ed.), *The Routledge Dyslexia Companion*, London, Routledge.

McLoughlin, D., Leather, C. and Stringer, P., (2002) *The Adult Dyslexic: Interventions and Outcomes*, London, Whurr Publishers.

McNaughton, S. (1995) *Patterns of emerging literacy: processes of development and transition*, Auckland: Oxford University Press.

McNaughton, S., Glynn, T. and Robinson, V. (1987) *Pause, Prompt and Praise: effective reading remedial tutoring*, Birmingham, Positive Products.

Marlin, R. (1997) School Improvement Conference (SIN), Leicestershire LEA, 20 February 1997.

Miles, T. R. (1983) *Bangor Dyslexia Test*, Cambridge, Learning Development Aids.

Mittler, P. (2001) *Working towards Inclusive education – Social Contexts*, London, David Fulton Publishers.

Mortimore, T. and Dupree, J. (2008) *Dyslexia Friendly Practice in the Secondary School*, Exeter, UK, Learning Matters Ltd.

Morton, J. and Frith, U. (1995) 'Causal Modelling: A structural approach to developmental psychopathology', in D. Cicchetti and D. J. Cohen (eds), *Manual of Developmental Psychopathology*, pp. 357–90, NY Psychological Assessment of Dyslexia: Wiley.

Mosley, J. (1996) *Quality Circle Time*, Cambridge, UK, LDA.

Nicolson, R. J. and Fawcett, A. J. (2008) Learning, Cognition and Dyslexia, in G. Reid, A. Fawcett, F. Manis and L. Siegel (2008) *The Sage Dyslexia Handbook*, London, Sage Publications.

Nicolson, R. I., Fawcett, A. J., and Dean, P. (2001) Developmental dyslexia: The cerebella deficit hypothesis, *Trends in Neurosciences*, 24(9), pp. 508–11.

Nicolson, R. I. and Fawcett, A. J. (1990) Automaticity: a new framework for dyslexia research?, *Cognition*, 35, pp. 159–82.

Nisbet, J. and Shucksmith, J. (1986) *Learning Strategies,* London, Routledge.

Northern Ireland Government (2002) Task Group Report on Dyslexia, 2002.

Norwich, B. (2009) How Compatible is the Recognition of Dyslexia with Inclusive Education? in G. Reid, G. Elbeheri, J. Everatt, J. Wearmouth, and D. Knight (eds), *The Routledge Dyslexia Companion*, UK, Routledge.

Norwich, B. and Lewis, A. (2001) Mapping a Pedagogy for Special Educational Needs, *British Educational Research Journal*, 27, 3?missing number?, 31331.

Norwich, B. and Lewis, A. (2005) 'How Specialized is Teaching Pupils with Disabilities and Difficulties?' in Lewis, A. and Norwich, B. (eds.) Special Teaching for Special Children? Pedagogies for Inclusion, Maidenhead: Open University Press.

Norwich, B. and Lewis, A. (2009) 'Mapping a Pedagogy for Special Educational Needs', in Fletcher-Campbell, F., Soler, J. and Reid, G. (eds), *Approaching Difficulties in Literacy Development: Assessment, Pedagogy and Programmes*, London, Sage.

Norwich, B., Goodchild, L. and Lloyd, S. (2001) Some Aspects of the Inclusion Index in Operation. *Support for Learning*, vol. 16, no. 4 pp. 156–61.

Oczkus, L. (2004) *Super Six Comprehension Strategies: 35 lessons and more for reading success*, MA, USA, Norwood, Christopher Gordon Publishers.

Palincsar, A. and Brown, A. (1984) 'Reciprocal Teaching of Comprehension Fostering and Comprehension Monitoring Activities'. *Cognition and Instruction*, 1(2), pp. 117–75.

Pavey, B. (2007) *The Dyslexia-Friendly Primary School: A Practical Guide for Teachers*, London, Sage Publications.

Peer L. and Reid, G. (eds) (2001) *Dyslexia – Successful Inclusion in the Secondary School*, London, David Fulton Publishers.

Portwood, M. (1999) *Developmental Dyspraxia, Identification and Intervention*. Second edition London: David Fulton.

Price, G. and Milgram, R. M. (1993) 'The Learning Styles of Gifted Adolescents Around the World. Differences and similarities', in R. M. Milgram, R. Dunn and G. E. Price (eds), *Teaching and Counselling Talented Adolescents: an international perspective*. Westport, CT, Praeger.

Pryce, L. and Gerber, P. (2007) Students with Dyslexia in Further and Higher Education: Perspectives and Perceptions, in G. Reid, A. Fawcett, F. Manis and L. Siegel, *The Dyslexia Handbook*, Sage Publications.

Pumfrey, P. D. and Reason, R. (1992) *Specific Learning Difficulties (Dyslexia): Challenges and Responses*, Windsor, Nelson, NFER.

QCA (2000) *The General Statement on Inclusion*, UK, DfEE.

Rack, J. (1994) 'Dyslexia: The phonological deficit hypothesis', in R. I. Nicolson and A. J. Fawcett (eds), *Dyslexia in Children: Multidisciplinary Perspectives*, Hemel Hempstead, Harvester Wheatsheaf.

Rack, J. (2010) Summary of the Rose Review Dyslexia Action: www.dyslexiaaction.org.uk/News/dr-john-racks-summary-of-the-rose-review (accessed January 2012).

Ranaldi, F. (2003) *Dyslexia and Design Technology*, London, David Fulton Publishers.

Reid, G. (2001a) 'Specialist Teacher Training in the UK: issues, considerations and future directions', in M. Hunter-Carsch (ed.), *Dyslexia, A Psychosocial Perspective*, pp. 252–262, London, Whurr Publications.

Reid, G. (2001b) 'Dyslexia, Metacognition and Learning Styles', in G. Shiel, and U. Ni Dhalaigh (eds), *Reading Matters: A Fresh Start Reading*, Dublin, Association of Ireland/National Reading Initiative.

Reid, G. (2003) *Dyslexia: A Practitioners Handbook* (3rd edn), Wiley.

Reid, G., Deponio, P. & Davidson-Petch, L. (2004) *Scotland-wide Audit of Education Authority Early Years Policies and Provision Regarding Specific Learning Difficulties (SpLD) and Dyslexia*. Edinburgh: SEED.

Reid, G. (2005) 'Learning Disabilities: The spectrum', in N. Jones (ed.), *Developing school provision for children with dyspraxia* (pp. 1–13), Thousand Oaks, CA: Sage Publications.

Reid, G. (2007) *Motivating Learners in the Classroom: Ideas and Strategies*, London, Sage Publications.

Reid, G. (2009) *Dyslexia: A Practitioners Handbook*, 4th edn, London, Wiley-Blackwell.

Reid, G. (2011) Paper presented at seminar series Australia and New Zealand March 2011 Compass Seminars, NZ.

Reid, G. and Came, F. (2009) 'Identifying and Overcoming the Barriers to Learning in an Inclusive Context', in G. Reid (ed.), *The Routledge Companion to Dyslexia* (pp. 193–202), New York, NY, Routledge.

Reid, G. and Given, B. (2000) 'Learning Styles', Reading, *BDA Handbook 2000*, BDA.

Reid, G. and Green, S. (2008) *The Teaching Assistant's Guide to Dyslexia*, London, Continuum Publications.

Reid, G. and Green, S. (2011) *100+ Ideas for Supporting Students with Dyslexia*, London, Continuum Publications.

Richardson, A. J. (2002) 'Dyslexia, Dyspraxia and ADHD – Can Nutrition Help?', Paper presented at Education Conference, Durham County Council, June 2002.

Riddell, S., Weedon, E., and Harris, N. (2012) 'Special and Additional Support Needs in England and Scotland – Current Dilemmas and Solutions', in L. Peer and G. Reid (eds), 2012, *Special Educational Needs: A Guide for Inclusive Practice*, London, Sage Publications.

Riddick, B. (2001) The Experiences of Teachers and Trainee Teachers Who Have Dyslexia. Paper presented at the Fifth International Conference, BDA, York, April.

Rose, J. (2006) The Rose Review into the Teaching of Reading, DfES, London (www.standards. dfes.gov.uk/rosereview/report).

Rose, J. (2009) Identifying and Teaching Children and Young People with Dyslexia and Literacy Difficulties, HMG UK (www.education.gov.uk/publications/eOrderingDownload/00659-2009 DOM-EN.pdf, accessed January 2012).

Sakellariadis, A. (2012) 'Inclusion and SEN: a dialogic inquiry into controversial issues', in L. Peer and G. Reid (eds), *Special Educational Needs: A Guide for Inclusive Practice*, London, Sage Publications.

Sayles, A. (2001) Paper presented at the Dyslexia Association of Ireland National Conference, University College, Dublin.

Scottish Executive (2002) 'Raising Attainment of Pupils with Special Educational Needs', *Interchange*, 67, 5.

Scottish Executive Education Department (2003) *Additional Support for Learning Act,* Edinburgh: The Stationery Office.

Scottish Executive (2005) *Supporting Children's Learning: Code of Practice*, Edinburgh: The Stationery Office.

Shiel, G. (2002) 'Literacy Standards and Factors Affecting Literacy: what national and international assessments tell us', in G. Reid and J. Wearmouth (eds), *Dyslexia and Literacy: Theory and Practice*, Wiley.

Silver, L. (2001) *Controversial Therapies – Perspectives*, vol. 27, No. 3 pp.1, 4, Baltimore, MD, USA, International Dyslexia Association.

Simpson, M. and Ure, J. (1993) *What's the Difference? A study of differentiation in Scottish secondary schools*, Aberdeen, UK, Aberdeen College.

Singleton, C. H. (2002) 'Dyslexia: Cognitive Factors and Implications for Literacy', in G. Reid and J. Wearmouth (eds), *Dyslexia and Literacy: Theory and Practice*, Wiley.

Singleton, C. H., Horne, J. K. and Thomas, K. V. (1999, 2002) *Lucid Adult Dyslexia Screening (LADS)*, Beverley, UK, Lucid Creative Limited.

Skidmore, D. (2004) *Inclusion: The dynamic of school development*, Buckingham: Open University Press.

Snowling, M. J. (2000) *Dyslexia* 2nd edn, Oxford, Blackwell.

Stein, J. (2008) 'The Neurobiological Basis of Dyslexia', in G. Reid, A. Fawcett, F. Manis and L. Siegel (2008), *The Sage Dyslexia Handbook*, London, Sage Publications.

Task Force on Dyslexia (2001) Report – Dublin: Republic of Ireland Government Publications. Available online at www.irlgov.ie/educ/pub.htm.

Thomas, G. and Vaughn, M. (2004) *Inclusive Education: Readings and Reflections*, Centre for Studies on Inclusive Education, Bristol, UK.

Thomson, M. (2008) Dyslexia and Inclusion in the Secondary School: cross curricular perspectives in Reid, G., Fawcett, A., Manis F. and Siegel, L., (2008). The Sage Dyslexia Handbook, London, Sage Publications UK.

Tod, J. Castle, F and Blamires, M. (1998) *Implementing Effective Practice*, London, David Fulton Publishers.

Tod, J. and Fairman, A. (2001) 'Individualized learning in a group setting', in L. Peer and G. Reid (eds), *Dyslexia – Successful Inclusion in the Secondary School*, London, David Fulton Publishers.

Tomlinson, S. (1985) 'The Expansion of Special Education', in *Oxford Review of Education* 11, 2, 15765.

Tonjes, M. (1988) 'Metacognitive Modelling and Glossing: two powerful ways to teach self responsibility', in Anderson, C. (ed.), *Reading: The abc and Beyond,* Basingstoke: Macmillan.

Topping, K. J. (1996) Parents and peers as tutors for dyslexic children. In Reid, G. (Ed.), *Dimensions of Dyslexia, Vol. 2 literacy, language and learning , Edinburgh*, Moray House Publications

Topping, K. J. (2001a) 'Peer and Parent Assisted Learning', in G. Shiel and U. Ni Dhalaigh (eds), *Reading Matters: A Fresh Start*, St Patrick's College, Dublin, Reading Association of Ireland/ National Reading Initiative, Education Research Centre.

Topping, K. J. (2001b) *Peer Assisted Learning, A Practical Guide for Teachers* (www.dundee. ac.uk/psychology/kjtopping/plearning.html), Cambridge, MA, Brookline Books.

Topping, K. J. (2001c) *Paired Reading, Spelling, and Writing: the handbook for teachers and parents*, London, Casell Education.

Topping, K. J. (2002) 'Paired Thinking, Developing Thinking Skills Through Structured Interaction with Peers, Parents and Volunteers', in G. Reid and J. Wearmouth (eds), *Dyslexia and Literacy: Theory and Practice*, Wiley.

Tunmer, W. E. and Chapman, J. (1996) 'A Developmental Model of Dyslexia. Can the construct be saved?' *Dyslexia*, 2(3), pp. 179–89.

Ulmer, C. and Timothy, M. (2001) 'How Does Alternative Assessment Affect Teachers' Practice? Two years later', Paper presented at the 12th European Conference on Reading, Dublin, Ireland, 1–4 July 2001.

US Government (2001) Full Funding of the Individuals with Disabilities Education Act (IDEA), 2001 Washington, USA.

Usmani, K. (1999) 'The Influence of Racism and Cultural Bias in the Assessment of Bilingual Children', *Educational and Child Psychology*, 16.3, pp. 44–54.

Velluntino, F., Fletcher, J., Snowling, M., and Scanlon, D. (2004) 'Specific Reading Disability (Dyslexia): what have we learned in the past four decades?', *Journal of Child Psychology and Psychiatry*, 45(1), 2–40.

Viall, J. T. (2000) 'High Stakes Assessment' *Perspectives*, (summer 2000 issue), vol. 26, no. 26, p.3, Baltimore, International Dyslexia Association.

Vygotsky, L. (1962) *Thought and Language* Cambridge, MA: MIT Press.

Vygotsky, L. S. (1978) *Mind in Society: The Development of Higher Psychological Processes,* Cambridge, MA, Harvard University Press.

Wagner, R. (2008) 'Rediscovering Dyslexia: New Approaches for Identification, Classification, and Intervention', in G. Reid, A. Fawcett, F. Manis and L. Siegel (eds), *The Sage Dyslexia Handbook,* London, Sage Publications.

Warnock, M. (2005) *Special Educational Needs: a new look*, Impact.

Warnock, M. (2012) Foreword to L. Peer and G. Reid (eds), 2012, *Special Educational Needs: A Guide for Inclusive Practice*, London, Sage Publications.

Wearmouth, J. (2001) 'Inclusion: Changing the Variables', in L. Peer and G. Reid (eds) *Dyslexia – Successful Inclusion in the Secondary School*, London, David Fulton Publishers.

Wearmouth, J. and Reid, G. (2002) Issues for Assessment and Planning of Teaching and Learning, in G. Reid and J. Wearmouth (eds), *Dyslexia and Literacy – Theory and Practice.* Wiley

Wearmouth, J., Soler, J. and Reid, G. (2002) *Meeting Difficulties in Literacy Development*, Routledge/Falmer.

Weedon, C. and Reid, G. (2001) *Listening and Literacy Index*, London, Hodder and Stoughton.

Weedon, C. and Reid, G. (2003) *Special Needs Assessment Portfolio*, London, Hodder and Stoughton.

Wendon, L. (1993) 'Literacy for Early Childhood: learning from the learners', *Early Child Development and Care*, 86, pp. 11–12.

West, T. G. (1992), second edition (2004) In the Mind's Eye. Visual Thinkers, Gifted People with Learning Difficulties, Computer Images and the Ironies of Creativity. Buffalo, NY, Prometheus Books.

West, T. G. (2009) *In the Mind's Eye: Visual Thinkers, Gifted People with Learning Difficulties, Computer Images and the Ironies of Creativity*, 2nd edn, Buffalo, NY, Prometheus Books.

Wilkins, A. (2004) *Reading Through Colour. How colour filters can reduce reading difficulty, eye strain and headaches*, Chichester, Wiley.

Williams, F. and Lewis, J. (2001), 'Geography and Dyslexia', in L. Peer and G. Reid (eds), *Dyslexia – Successful Inclusion in the Secondary School*, London, David Fulton Publishers.

Wilson, J. and Frederickson, N. (1995) 'Phonological Awareness Training: an evaluation', *Educational and Child Psychology*, 12(1), pp. 68–79.

Wray, D. (1994) *Literacy and Awareness*, London, Hodder & Stoughton.

Wray, D. (2002) 'Metacognition and Literacy' in G. Reid and J. Wearmouth (eds) *Dyslexia and Literacy: Theory and Practice*, Wiley.

Wolf, M. and O'Brien, B. (2001), 'On Issues of Time, Fluency and Intervention', in A. Fawcett (ed.), *Dyslexia, Theory and Good Practice*, London, Whurr Publications.

Young, G. and Browning, J. (2004) Learning Disability/Dyslexia and Employment, in G. Reid and A. Fawcett (eds) *Dyslexia in Context, Research, Policy and Practice*. London, Whurr

Index